The Anatomy of
Wake-up Calls
Volume 1

The Anatomy of Wake-up Calls Volume 1

WHAT SHALL BE DONE

Dr. Feridoun Shawn Shahmoradian

THE ANATOMY OF WAKE-UP CALLS VOLUME 1
WHAT SHALL BE DONE

iUniverse books may be ordered through booksellers or by contacting:

iUniverse
1663 Liberty Drive
Bloomington, IN 47403
www.iuniverse.com
1-800-Authors (1-800-288-4677)

ISBN: 978-1-4917-7988-0 (sc)
ISBN: 978-1-4917-7989-7 (hc)
ISBN: 978-1-4917-7987-3 (e)

Library of Congress Control Number: 2015917037

Print information available on the last page.

iUniverse rev. date: 10/22/2015

Preface

This collection of essays may seem at first to be a "shotgun" approach to some kind of strange philosophy, covering everything from terrorism to God to the afterlife to freedom, sex, money, avoiding being duped, and many more seemingly disparate subjects. The connecting link might not seem apparent at first, but my goal is for the reader to begin to see the patterns and wisdom woven throughout, all of which presents a distillation of a lifetime of observing the world through the eyes of a deeply spiritual person and thinker whose perspective is also that of a tenth degree black belt and trainer of black belts.

This is not a novel or book to read straight through. My intent is for the essays to be read individually, one at a time, like a devotional of sorts, and then pondered for elements that might be taken for inspiration or further research into facets of subjects that might pique the reader's interest. Each stands alone and so can be read in any order. Take a rest between each and think about your reaction, whether agreement of disagreement, and why such thoughts or feelings emerged. I believe that such an approach will result in deepening your thinking and widening your perspective, and who can honestly say that wouldn't be a benefit to them?

On a personal note, I was born in Iran but have lived in the U.S. since age 18. I was educated in America, obtaining an electronic engineering degree and two master's degrees, and my early interest in martial arts turned into a lifetime pursuit of excellence. After publishing my first book, *Mind Fighter: The Invisible Defender*, which primarily describes "The Forty Beacons of Self-Defense," I wanted to share on a more personal, heart-felt level, which took the form of this collection of essays that represent a lifetime of intense reading, research, pondering, weighing, sifting, and discerning. I am profoundly appreciative that you have honored me by journeying for this time into my world. I trust the journey will be fruitful and helpful for you, especially in a world that grows increasingly more insecure and dangerous, ironically, to human life and is in desperate need of souls like you who have a sincere desire to improve themselves, sharpen their thinking, and become better human beings.

— Dr. Feridoun (Shawn) Shahmoradian

Killing in the Name of Allah (God)

You maim and disfigure, you murder, execute, rape, and do the most heinous crimes without any legal consequences whatsoever. You violently abuse and humiliate innocent people, you barbarically torture your opponents and appallingly seek revenge with no mercy, and you take what is not yours. You force yourself on people's lives and their decency, and you confiscate their possessions to make them *halal* (to cleanse them)—all in the name of Allah.

Then, as you wash your hands of the blood after horrifyingly exercise your evil acts and satanic behavior, you start to pray to Allah towards Mecca, so shamelessly expecting to be promoted in heaven and earth, and rewarded in his name for your good deeds. You act as if the omnipotent God, our omnipresent Father, is somehow the predecessor or successor of Genghis Khan, hovering over the innocent as if he were the commander of hatred and suffering. You act as if our God is a warlord, demonic and ferocious, extending his arm through your bloodied sleeves, upholding celestial rules and the laws of divinity through violence. You then refer to Quran Karim like it is a written manual on how to act demonically and a roadmap to actual hell, decimating the children of the almighty Allah, and making the believers to question his righteousness and the validity of his mercy and compassion on humanity.

May God curse you as you so viciously and abhorrently intrude on people's sovereignty, killing and robbing them of their life, wealth, and happiness? Even the barbarian Genghis adhered to his constitution's laws of Yasa, which forbad the killing or maiming of those who surrendered. He also spared and forbad hurting women, the elderly, and children, but you who call yourself "ISIS" and attack innocent bystanders, capturing whomever is not in your guild. Then you eliminate them, raping, torturing, burning alive, or beheading them execution style, all the while loudly and proudly declaring Allah that is great. Seriously, do you truly believe you will not rot and burn in hell, claiming and accrediting to his holy name your beastly behaviors and savagery?

The truth is, you are nothing more than a messenger of evil, just like Hitler or Genghis Khan. Isn't what you are doing the same, if not worse—and all in the name of Allah? At least Genghis had the courage and was courteous enough to believe in his fellow commanders and soldiers, when he said in his famous quote, "One arrow can be broken, but many arrows are indestructible." He believed in unity and respected his alliance with his friends and supporters.

Your demons are practically incompetent of any unity, and the world has witnessed when you so cowardly put other naïve and shallow-minded followers with a herd-like mentality at risk of suicide in the killing of helpless and innocent people. You act as judge, jury, prosecutor, and executioner, with no fear from Allah, blindly hoping that what will await you in heaven, in the land of Oases, are plenty of virgins, artesian wells with sweet water, and everything ambient with streams of milk and honey. You don't have an inkling, nor are you even aware of the laws of the universe that have been demonstrated trillions and trillions of times—"what goes around comes around"—and you and your colleagues, who are nothing but a pile of amoral dirt, are surely no exception, and bound to rot in hell with the utmost of punishment, and may the angel of death be upon you.

If you are foolish enough to hope for the reward of martyrdom, rest assured that this is not going to happen. Your vile message clearly institutes fear, cruelty, and injustice, and deviates diametrically from the righteous path, and even from what is human. This makes you lower in rank than humans, and more in tune with the most vicious animals. The simple truth is that anyone in good conscious and with wisdom should ask you and your kind, "Just how far someone's stupidity can go before waking up to an inch of humanity?"

Terrorism—Its Ramification and Remedies

Terrorism is a satanic and inhumane thought, the aim of which is to spread fear by conducting psychological warfare. It adamantly tries to create terrorist phobia, uncertainty, and chaos, and to divide humanity. It grows and matures when it generates propaganda and feeds on the twin corpses of illiteracy and ignorance. It has been said that propaganda only has to be popular, and it has to accommodate itself to the comprehension of the least intelligent of those whom it seeks to reach. Thus, it makes sure to search out and to prey on naïve and impoverished individuals who are stricken with a host of misfortunes.

Their dire circumstances make them easy prey, because they are adamant in finding the answer to their destitute desperation, with their only hope in life to reach happiness in the afterlife via heaven above. It is understandable that those of such criterion and short sightedness, with confused emotions and frustrated minds will fall trap in the corollary of ugly and intricate games being played on them. The con is complete when they foolishly become a full-blown terrorist, ready to die for someone else's evil cause. They gullibly adopt behavior that doesn't mind inflicting pain and suffering on others, and also self, and they unwittingly embrace an extremist view on life. Then, fully equipped with impulsive attributes, they commit to killing themselves and others, having first been brainwashed and then trained in covert actions with resoluteness in camouflaging and sudden unwarned attacks. These fanatics are the end result when seeds of stupidity have had the perfect conditions in which to grow in the fertile ground of desperate people with nothing to lose.

These soldiers of misfortune are wretchedly conditioned to induce psychological fear, and to create panic and execute harm where it is not expected. Their fearlessness and commitment to achieve their objectives stems out of being willing to sacrifice their lives and valuing what they believe in beyond this life. These self-destructive tendencies occur not because they are devoted to their masters, the manipulating minds behind their delusions, but they truly believe in the nonsense rhetoric with which they are being indoctrinated. This is where the real danger lies, with the end result of almost daily news reports about more inhumane terrorism, devastating scenes, evil acts, and despicable atrocities.

The response of humanity is to either lose hope or to fight back, and since the terrorists want people to lose hope, it is also the best reason to fight back and to absolutely deny them their malicious and beastly intent. According to Ban Ki Moon, fascism and terrorism believe that, "To demoralize the enemy from within by surprise, terror, sabotage, assassination, this the war of the future." An insidious and cowardly act such as murdering innocent people should warn humanity to **wake up** and realize that to be idle is to embolden ruthless terrorists to unleash more mental, physical, and financial destruction. And I say "We ought to know in a hunting ground sitting ducks will be slathered." Terrorism is a significant threat to peace and security, prosperity, and people." But waking up and being aware will only solve part of the problem. What must be done is to stop the holy grail of this madness played on humanity. It is crucial to take away what these terrorist feed on, which is victims with unbearable situations who are willing to sacrifice themselves while murdering innocents, simply because they have nothing to lose and have bought into the propaganda of a glorious life after death.

These invokers, these mercenaries, these messengers of death capitalize on how true Muslims are treated since they are dominated by poverty because their resources of trillions are unfairly exploited and pillaged; thus, the Muslim faith ironically is endangered by those falsely claiming its name. Willing dupes responding to the terrorist game plan is essential to its survival—which is the most urgent reality that needs to be dealt with through proper technology, advanced thinking, and policies rendered by experts in communication, as well as adequate funding. Terrorism must become a bad dream of the past, which will happen only by taking these culprits' support away, exhausting them of their most critical resources, and stripping them of them followers. There are other treatments available for curing this cancerous tumor rather than through wars and violence. No one is going to cure terrorism and make peace, trustworthiness, and good will by destroying innocent lives and by dropping bombs all over them.

Using the terrorist recruiters' playbook against them, people will believe in you when you give them the basic necessities of living of which they have been deprived—food, shelter, clean water, sanitation, medicine, doctors and hospitals, electricity, employment, and education. It is common knowledge that the mouth being fed is less likely to bite the hand that is feeding it. Your sincere motive with a little patience on a global scale has the potential to nonviolently wipe out terrorism by simply **waking people up**. Noam Chomsky wisely said, "Everybody is worried about stopping terrorism; well there is a really easy way—stop participating in it." Prominent human right activist Shirin Ebadi said, "When a person is humiliated, when his rights are being violated, and he does not have proper education, naturally he gravitates toward terrorism." This needs to be an international, grassroots movement educating the masses, which has the power to overpower the terrorists' slick propaganda, for example, "The Muslim religion is being targeted as vile." The truth is that the relative minority of Muslim terrorists has created both the targeting of all Muslims as vile, and the sympathy for the vast majority of innocent Muslim adherents. They are hiding in plain sight and calling the devious shots all the while hiding behind the true Muslim faith like a righteous shield. Exposing these lies on a grand scale will undo what has been propagated, which has helped them to lure in masses of simple-minded, naïve, idealistic youth who either do not have the ability or have never taken the time to think for themselves. Since these recruits easily fall in the terrorists' spider web traps, they quickly become brainwashed into believing the terrorists' carefully crafted but completely deceptive mantras. The new mantra should not be, "The Muslim faith is not to blame for terrorism" (thus concealing terrorists within the Muslim umbrella); rather, it should more accurately be, "The minority of Muslims are causing all the trouble" (which inherently exonerates the innocent masses).

We are all doing the best we can to obey the laws of our respective lands and to uphold a free society where balance in everyone's welfare is not to be overlooked, and where dignity and human rights, justice, freedom, and democracy include everyone with no exception. The time has come, however, for the good people of the world to set aside pride and complacency and to reach out to lost and confused around us in good faith and to show them that there is a better way.

We are in possession of so many countless atomic, bacterial, chemical, neurological, and other poisonous weaponries, that if we were to sneeze the whole world would practically goes to ashes, ending what we know as planet earth—it is so incomprehensibly scary. Howard Zenn wisely asked, "How can you have a war on terrorism when the war itself is terrorism?" That is why it is extremely vital to reach those who are dull in comprehension, and to make them aware that we are already in a deep hole and must stop digging. Again, I must reiterate the importance of education and becoming enlightened with the reality of what kind of animals are we dealing with here.

Knowing facts can be quite resourceful in dealing with characters who are ignorant but who possess the power to cause irreparable damage. The favorite weapon of choice for terrorists is to emotionally prey on their victims, deceitfully reminding them of their duty to Allah and to desperate and deprived fellow Muslims everywhere. They also motivate recruits with a bare minimum of financial incentive, which is only to guarantee their immediate family will survive when they are gone. And then of course there is the empty promise of heaven, with all the rewards of the Oasis, and infinite streams of milk and honey, with a never-ending supply of the most beautiful girls, all of whom happen to remain virgins at all time, the best musicians, and other heavenly entertainment beyond anyone's imagination.

So, one can see the appeal of heavenly rewards, should someone convincingly entice those with a callow mentality to believe and accept such grandiose descriptions as truth, to encourage a steady stream of newcomers to fight in the charlatan's war. Hence, these terror groups are fervently brainwashing potential recruits with the positives of martyrdom, i.e., financial securities for their families, a ticket to heaven and glorious promises of the afterlife, with eternal lasciviousness and fulfillment of all their needs and wishes. Of course, the truth is they are fortifying, strengthening, and expanding their brand of secular Islam with the sacrificed bodies of hapless victims of manipulation.

In the meantime, is it really too much to ask to fight this game head on—at the manipulation level of recruiting—and not after the recruits attack and are sacrificed, by fueling the fire through bombing innocent civilians and then counting them as "collateral damage"? This only infuriates their sons, daughters, and immediate families, relatives, and others to join these terror networks—which is exactly what the terrorists are after, more bloodshed. Instead, by constructively investing in their life and future to bypass their hopeless situation, which makes one so gullible as to believe it is better to die by a detonated bomb rather than by a gradual, natural death. It would of inestimable, global value to educate and inspire potential converts so they could discern between fact and fiction, and not fall into the trap baited with such mirages of deception and hypocrisy created by the terrorists.

Is it too much to ask those who intervene with warfare not to take control of their oil and gas, and not to exploit other valuable natural and human resources? And if you must take from them, at least to spend it constructively and not on your weapon of choice to kill them all, including helpless women, children, elderly and youth, rather than educating and subsidizing their poor way of life where they can be integrated into the system? You have the ability to inspire them to believe in modern society, and to believe in your compassion and humanity, promoting a better world for the sake of goodness and God. Pope Francis said, "Human rights are not violated only by terrorism, repression, assassination, but also by unfair economic structures that create huge inequalities."

Are they not entitled to some financial recovery to be devoted to their wellbeing, and into improving their life of literacy and education, health and hygiene, making them less vulnerable to these fake devotees of Allah (God the Almighty) whose only intent is to turn them into ruthless killers, rewarding them only with martyrdom? We have the resources to broaden their perspective about a healthy life, and to encourage them to value life, and not to be vulnerable and brainwashed by any other cultural tendency they might entertain—and especially not to be lured in by the myths of the religious extremists. They need to know and respect human values and to learn that we are all from the same family under God. Above all, they need to be taught that it did not come from God or his holy book to murder innocent people and then be rewarded for it.

Instead, they need to be accommodated with an uplifting spirit who can help them to resolve their differences via peaceful means, and to identify and weed out any rough and violent behavior. By being told the truth, perhaps they will not be so easily inspired with the promises of heaven and its amenities orated to them by the angels of death. These impulsive outbursts of manipulated violence can be cured and forgotten via compassion and constructive education and literacy. Viable remedies can only be materialized, however, if we could collectively discard our pride and prejudice and to prove that what is preached about human rights, justice, freedom, and democracy is true. Rather than being brainwashed that Jews and Christians are their enemy, they need to learn that they invented justice and freedom, and deserve the credit for it, not unjust death. Was it not this trend of genuine heavenly thought that aroused the nations to fight against the fascist and ruthless dictatorial systems with much sacrifice, before, during, and after World War II, and that this still is the case today?

I believe we have the potential to convince even the most jaded of enemies to have a second thought, to doubt their own vicious kind, and to be inclined to a change of heart. What I am saying is that it is possible for a better government to rule without prejudice, existing only to profit humanity. I believe it is possible without violence, but by peaceful means; otherwise, what is the difference between evil-inspired terrorism and good-inspired terrorism? Doesn't terrorism essentially mean killing, maiming, and destroying innocent people's lives, destruction of their hopes and belongings, no matter who is perpetrating it, and no matter for what cause? Thus, what do you have if you destroy in the name of freedom, justice, human rights, democracy, liberty, and the pursuit of happiness? Such behavior is sure to fall into the abyss of God's justice, no different than the original terrorism that inspired those who in turn would annihilate them.

It should be noted that unleashed greed and pride can spread trouble far and wide like an epidemic disease, and such evil potential should be watched over. We cannot go back to the barbaric dark ages where the last glimmer of hope and societal civility was extinguished. Let us pray that the grace of God instead would be sustain human life through peace and godly compassion. This culture of animosity should predominantly be replaced with the most effective weapon of choice, which is to have these victim's interests at heart and sincerely care, boycotting their recruiters and denying the masterminds of wicked conduct. Perhaps I will be categorized as an idealist and utopia, but is a proven fact that people armed with not much more than passion have conquered the world in the course of our human history.

This malady of thought can be overcome. There is a saying, "only death is with no solution" if destined. It is clear that when reason and logic are absent, then emotional impulses tend to kick in and affect the outcome for the worse. We should not behave absentmindedly toward the lessons that history has painfully taught. Many tyrants have played on people's emotions and have successfully strummed the music of demagoguery, achieving their devious goals, like Hitler appealing to racial fears, provoking people's feelings to want to mercilessly wipe out an entire nation of people, simply because they were not from the Arian race. Stalin and others alike preyed on people's emotions in the name of "equality" and "socialism," unjustly killing millions of "unequal" members of society in the process. Today, equally manipulative, hardcore terrorists victimize other gullible human souls from among their own peoples in the name of "Allah" to fulfill their inhumane ideas. So many other lessons of human history should not to be overlooked, and instead should be remembered and publicized in order to help repudiate and to stop further aggression from these abhorrent and beasty personalities. We need to restructure our thoughts and deeds, to give priority to defending innocent lives wherever there are crimes against humanity; and to reincarnate a new human image that is compatible with the twentieth first century in achieving an era of civility of mind and manner. Such a culture would practice our collective higher self, and would utilize our collective good conscious wherever it would be needed to lift up the helpless and the unprotected.

What make sense is to see how outsourcing and corporate financial might have been so widespread, reaching to even the most remote places of the planet, to the point where it is a game changer now. Since cultural differences and perhaps people consciousness about natural and human resources being exploited make people understandably angry, wisdom should inspire us to take preventive measure to stop and to trouble shoot such things. We have the ability to become more accommodating and helpful in supporting the livelihoods of conquered people, making this a world where everyone can belong. The same as one's long-term investment can be more prosperous, so meaningful and constructive behavior in today's wartime climate can yield long-term positive results. This in turn can bring true meaning to a win-win situation, which also can mitigate and perhaps someday it might truly become a reality to terminate terrorist activities in their entirety.

The incentive to act in one accord is to prevent terrorism from becoming an even worse global epidemic, and to save countless people from the malice of poverty and slavery to the conquering terrorists. We must reinforce our allies to fight more wisely against those who mean to uphold terrorism, and to seize good opportunities to stir up the crowds in the name of needless poverty and desperation. We are in an era of awakened consciousness where the good people of the world condemn colonialism, racism, and other such behaviors, who instead contribute humanism, liberty, justice, and rights for all. The above changes are a must in order to stop supporting repressive and autocratic regimes. If this happens, it will induce a much friendlier global atmosphere, and the countries where our presence is necessary will not resent us. This should certainly help in nullifying terrorism's effort in causing damage, and perhaps make it more difficult to isolate and dupe others to support their cause. My ideal would direct everyone toward a "no boundaries" attitude where a one-world government could rule, destined to make everyone accepted and protected by decent laws that would be more in line with the twenty-first century and far away from a dark ages mentality.

It is vibrantly important to listen to those who talk about the role of philanthropy to shorten and to mitigate the problems of income inequality and to prevent inequities where poverty could push people to their limit and into the arms of seasoned terrorists to become abused and taken advantage of. Of course, there are other motivating factors that play roles, but if the issue of poverty is relatively resolved, where people could afford basic education, basic health, food, and shelter, and have secure employment, which are self-perpetuating since these people then become productive members of society. Such a plan surely would remedy more problems than boycotts and denying leverage to the enemies of freedom, democracy, and human rights.

Thoughts About God

The most important self-defense move that you can ever make is to believe in and seek God. In a consumer-oriented society that is intensely materially based, profit is becoming the sole purpose and is replacing God in people's hearts. It is as if God exists today only as an empty shell with no kernel. It is more urgent than ever to truly and sincerely call upon the omnipotent, omnipresent God and seek to know him with all you might. The conventional method of reaching God, as practiced by some charlatans, is nothing more than a joke; it is only about getting more dollars into their pockets. This form of practice uses scare tactics and sleazy maneuvers to fool and undermine people's normal rational thought.

This happens even though this is the twenty-first century, and most people and civilized nations have become quite sophisticated, and most naturally question such phony religious practices. God does not deserve this kind of treatment, and neither do his true children. Yet we see many instances of those who preach such a wrong message about God and they should, in this writer's opinion, be dealt no mercy. When you are spiritually broken and in need of spiritual shelter and help, and you take refuge with those who claim to be men of God—and then receive nothing but more trouble, it would take a strong, sane mind not to curse and deny God.

We should discern that such false prophets are just more hypocrites who live among us. Their corrupt deeds spiritually kill and maim people's spirits until there is no remedy for them other than deliverance by the true God. He is not the cause of human misery; rather, the causes are in large part from those who bludgeon others in the name of God. Never before has the existence of God been so well substantiated, with so much hardcore support and proof, all of which is heavily backed by the collective sciences of reason, philosophy, archaeology, linguistics, and every branch of scientific knowledge. Yet so many are becoming remote islands, getting further and further away from the vicinity of their maker, no longer tethered to or encompassed within his territory.

People of high moral fiber are asking why so many nations, steeped in education and immersed in civility of mind and manner, have such rampant and pandemic levels of crime and wrongdoing. Catastrophes are everywhere, as we are bombarded on all sides by disasters, wars, hunger, and so many scenarios that are void of tranquility and serenity of mind. Each and every day our livelihood is questioned and hanging by a thread. In such an environment, the lower self is praised so much that it cannot be changed without God's help. This is only possible if people sincerely believed in the almighty God, not by acting double faced and being hypocritical.

Reason can and should be a beacon helping mankind to reach enlightenment and in convincing man to know God not with superstition, but via thorough understanding and logic. Further, we should know that the principle of causality states that if there is no intelligence in the design and the effect, there could not be intelligence in the cause. Therefore, if there is intelligence in man, there must be intelligence in man's cause. It is of solidified reasoning that a being must exist as some form of mass in space and time. No creator can be part of what was created or within it. It defies all sorts of reasoning and logic. God, our maker, does not visibly exist in created space, matter, or time as we know and perceive them. Still, some theorists ignorantly inquire, "Where is God? Show him to me," or "I went to space and didn't see God anywhere." We are not products of chance; we are intelligently designed, and many if not the majority of scientists agree with this.

A principle of modern science emerged in 1980 called the anthropic principle, the basic thrust of which is that human existence by accident or chance is not valid. Believing otherwise invalidates all laws of chemistry, conservation, angular momentum, and every other scientific law, such as physics, conservation of electric charges, and so on. To believe that matter is uncaused is to believe against and discard all the known immutable laws of science and principles of the universe. Dealing with conservation of matter and energy would be nothing but an obtuse, insane approach to reason. Unless directed by some being endowed with knowledge and Intelligence, whatever lacks intelligence cannot intentionally move toward an end. As the arrow that is shot to its mark by the archer, anything worth living has a purpose and is here to accomplish its goal and objective.

These facts can be seen and witnessed throughout nature. The whole is made up of the parts, and if the parts have destiny and purpose, then logic dictates that the whole that comprises these parts also has a destiny and purpose. To say we come from nowhere and we are going nowhere—that it is all just an accident—simply does not add up and is both wrong and contradictory. Even the famous phrase "the survival of the fittest" presupposes the arrival of the fit. If Darwinists wish to maintain this purely biological theory, that the entire vast order around us is the result of random chance and random changes, then they are also saying that nothing of any empirical evidence can ever be confirmed. And no empirical science can be demonstrated since science and experience are two intertwined and interdependent twins, where one without the other is just not possible. It is like evolution, which is defined by Merriam Webster as, "the process of change in certain direction," which is nothing but a journey. What common sense should unfold is that moving to any direction should encompass purpose and destination. Anything evolutionary should be directed toward a purpose and completeness no matter how long it takes, and how further apart from beginning to end; it means a process needing to reach its destination and to complete its journey. Similarly, noting the "big bang grand explosion," I thought anything explosive results in simple destruction, which brings about predictable disorder and chaos, instead of order, intelligence, and complexity.

Not that I believe that the "big bang" did not happen, but what I believe is it occurred under an infinitely intelligent and powerful designer, and that it happened under God's control. Thus, I believe he created such an orderly, extremely disciplined, and superbly complex universe as ours out of a disorderly situation, where it appeared that nothing intelligent could possibly reside. Thinking that such a deliberate hand had to be responsible for making this magical orderly cosmos from an utterly a destructive situation, MIT physicist Vera Kistiakowsky said, "The exquisite order displayed by our scientific understanding of the physical world calls for the divine." Referencing God, Thomas Aquinas argued for him being the "unmoved mover." We know that there is motion in the world, and it follows that whatever is in motion has been moved by something else. This other thing, in turn, must have been moved by something, and so on.

To avoid an infinite regression, we must posit a first and a prime mover that is beyond our space, matter, and time. That ultimate, prime, or unmoved mover is our God. Hawkins, arguably today's most famous physicist, does not believe in a God that he cannot see. Yet he claims, ironically, that the unseen force of gravity is what keeps life and the universe grounded and is also the root cause of existence. For those who do not have to see God to believe in him, gravity is merely an unseen force that is subject to God's power, as are all the other unseen forces in the world such as electromagnetic, atomic energy, and so on. One has to wonder why it is so difficult for Hawkins to see the similar glory of the unseen God as the root cause of the infinite complexity of existence and the obviously intelligent design of the universe.

With all due respect to Hawkins, his is nothing but a vainglorious statement, uttered by a fallible man who is willfully blind to the obvious on all sides—as well as both macro- and micro-realities, both of which are beyond human perception. Only God provides the best explanation for the DNA codes contained in each human cell and controlling the design and function of life on earth. Antony Flew, a professor of philosophy, former atheist, author, and debater, stated, "It now seems to me that the finding of some more than fifty years of DNA research have provided materials for a new enormously powerful argument to design." Only God provides the best explanation for the absolute complexity inherent in every element of the universe—including cosmological, planetary, chemical, biological, physical, atomic, natural, electromagnetic, and gravity forces—all interconnected with utmost precision and balance to be optimal to support human life.

Alexander Polyakov, a Soviet mathematician, affirmed, "We know that nature is described by the best of possible mathematics because God created it." It should be obvious that no mathematics is possible without order. The impossible alternative is that every one of our highly complex inventions, such as binary code, sophisticated and powerful computers, and wireless technology, occurred without any programming, testing, debugging, or planning. This impossible alternative, called the theory of random chance, holds that all our modern, engineering marvels are not the result of intelligent design but simply fell into place accidentally—and it is all without purpose or meaning but simply exists infinitely, as it always has, meandering endlessly and vacuously. The meaning of vacuous is empty, insane, or stupid, which ironically describes the theory.

However illogical, improbable, or impossible, many have subscribed to this theory—despite the cognitive dissonance that inert, random matter is neither self-perpetuating, nor self-aware, nor capable of creating intelligence, purpose, or meaning. While it is true that all the phenomenological and biological systems could not and did not take a huge and unseen leap from simple too complex to maturity, they are all under the influence of and are being conducted with intentional, gradual effort and purpose. Everything is part of a guided process and forward-looking instruction.

One can only produce nature and invent science from an orderly cosmos and scientific blueprint; one can only create human complexity from a discipline-coded and superior source of life. Nothing orderly and disciplined, such as the theory of relativity or other vital scientific laws and principles, could have come from a disorderly, chaotic, randomized universe. If physics is the heart and the soul of science, as physicists and scientists claim, then they are more aware than anyone that mathematics—the ultimate in logic and order—is the heart and the soul of physics. It is a vital principle that applied mathematics reasoning and logic produces harmony.

It is a no brainer that human life and everything that surrounds and sustains it could not and did not happen randomly but rather by intelligent design. Cosmologists Zehavi and Dekel concur, "This type of universe, however, seems to require a degree of fine tuning of the initial conditions that is in apparent conflict with common wisdom." It is only another baby step of logic that the universe with such a conscious, intelligent, and disciplined creator not only brought order, balance, beauty, harmony, logic, and infinite complexity into being, but also has an eternal purpose and meaning for human existence. We ought to know God is not inseparable from our spirit and soul and our good conscious.

God is the silent voice within you and me and every nuance of existence. Beyond the known micro and macro particles of our infinite universe is not a matter of any kind, according to "positivism doctrine" and other similar beliefs, who so naively claim, "I must see it to believe it." If an intelligent, ordering, and creating God is not behind all this that is before our eyes, including the powerful eyes of telescopes and microscopes, the vast majority of which exceeds all of our intelligent and perceptive powers combined, then who or what is? In reality, his spirit is both beyond and within the mind and body of universe, and we are indeed fortunate to be the proprietors, relatively speaking, of a single drop from the infinite ocean of his holy soul. The truth is that when we are being enlightened, considered, and compassionate; when we have kindness and love, empathy, pity, courage, self-sacrifice, forgiveness, piety, faithfulness, and patience; when we are philanthropic, truthful, seeking freedom, and democratic; when we pursue equity, justice, and peace—only then do we feel God. As you can see, there really is no sane choice but to practice your higher self, where the spirit of goodness directs you to do no evil and become pleasantly righteous in all that you do. It is then, when you are in a realm engulfed with the spirit of the almighty God, the omnipotent, omniscient, and omnipresent father, that you become truly human as he intended when he created you.

Grand Design or Grand Accident?

It is because of a lack of knowledge and the blind leading the blind that causes some people to stand their ground and profess their dogmatic claims, making them delusional to not realize the essential concept of "mind versus matter." Our human brain is comprised only of human matter, but they so willfully try to mimic and build artificial human brains in laboratories. This is practical vanity from the start, but they do not realize their efforts are futile. Human brains come with resident super complex software that is not apart from their cosmic programming, which complies with the energy of the universe. Those who attempt to recreate what cannot be recreated do not fathom that it is an extra-terrestrial and a meta-physical domain that rejects any brain hardware manufactured by mortals because, ironically, the human brain is beyond human comprehension.

The questions that persist for most are, "What is the nature of consciousness?" "Why are we here?" "Is there a soul"? "Why are things the way they are?" "Where did we come from?" "Where are we going?" There are so many other unanswered questions that are beyond the limit and the propensity of any scientific discovery or endeavor to correctly answer. No matter how advanced in science and technology humanity becomes, any attempt in creating "artificially intelligence" will be doomed to failure and disappointment, since our human intelligence is linked to and is part of the cosmic intelligence where its creator does not operate within matter, space, and time as we know it.

It is the world of the unseen that surreptitiously maneuvers the quantum world, the world of string theory, and other subatomic particles. When Greek philosophers Leucippus and Democritus first discovered the concept of the atom in the 5th century B.C.E., they were wrong when they claimed it was the smallest particle known, which obviously was a great discovery, but we didn't know at the time was not the whole truth. Of course, we now know the smallest particle of matter is known as a "quark," which is claimed by many prominent physicist and contemporary scientific scholars. In 1904, Sir Isaac Newton presented his groundbreaking laws of motion, which are three physical laws that together laid the foundation for classical mechanics. They describe the relationship between a body and the forces acting upon it, and its motion in response to said forces. They have been expressed in several different ways over nearly three centuries, and can be summarized as follows:

First law: When viewed in an inertial reference frame, an object either remains at rest or continues to move at a constant velocity, unless acted upon by an external force.

Second law: The vector sum of the forces F on an object is equal to the mass M of that object multiplied by the acceleration vector A of the object: $F = ma$.

Third law: When one body exerts a force on a second body, the second body simultaneously exerts a force equal in magnitude and opposite in direction on the first body.

At the time, these laws were believed to represent the whole truth regarding the laws of motion, but they were not, despite their outstanding importance and the fact that many vital scientific discoveries were and continue to be based on them. Einstein broke into new territory, which exposed the limitations of Newton's laws.

Albert Einstein (March 14, 1879 to April 18, 1955) was a German-born theoretical physicist whose work is also known for its influence on the philosophy of science. He developed the general theory of relativity, one of the two pillars of modern physics (alongside quantum mechanics). Einstein is best known in popular culture for his mass–energy equivalence formula E = mc2 (which holds the distinctive title of "the world's most famous equation"). He received the 1921 Nobel Prize in Physics for his "services to theoretical physics," in particular, his discovery of the law of the photoelectric effect, a critical step in the evolution of quantum theory. In his thinking, Newton's mechanics were no longer enough to reconcile the laws of classical mechanics with the laws of the electromagnetic field.

The applicability of Einstein's general theory of relativity is to the large-scale structure of the universe, about which scientists are looking for one theory that can explain everything, which is known simply as "the theory of everything." This should be quite encouraging, and I believe we can rest assured that thousands of other, so to speak, reliable theories will materialize, pushing us ever further in our evolutionary quest for reaching the whole truth. But it will be naïve to think man can ever decipher the whole truth, unless we can reach beyond and outside of matter, space, and time, which I certainly believe is impossible. This would also answer why we are here, and many other intricate questions that to date have been beyond our understanding. As has been said throughout human history, only God knows everything, so if we want ultimate answers, we must seek him.

In our search for heaven, we are clearly helpless to reach the whole truth, with even having the most complex and advanced telescopes, since they are not as efficient as they need to be to reveal the entire magic that lies in the heaven above, the sheer magnanimity of which should be appreciated. It is about this sacred prevalent energy, electromagnetic forces, gravity, and all the tiny and colossal atomic forces that are invisible and poetically potent, all of which we take for granted when doing our everyday chores via internet, cells, digital gadgets, computers, TV, satellite, and so many other inventions born of technology making our life easier.

So it is all about the unseen world that orchestrates and rules the world we see. Again, with all due respect, Mr. Hawkins and his followers say that gravity is what made life possible, and he rightfully should be credited for any of his genuine scientific discoveries; but in my view, he goes too far when he denies God, which I believe also should trouble any logical person. Mr. Hawkins simply does not acknowledge that we only know the effect of such invisible forces like gravity. Moreover, the laws of gravity can perhaps explain many things scientifically, even possibly including how the universe was made, but it simply cannot be accepted that a finite, inanimate force, gravity, made the infinite, animated universe, and I have already addressed the logical impossibility that man and everything known to man is the result of random chance. In his book, *The History of Time,* Mr. Hawkins states, "The universe came to existence from nothingness," adding, "it was made by gravity." The question should be, which one is it? Did we come out of nothing, or was the universe created by something, which something Mr. Hawkins believes is gravity?

He also states that time began with the big bang explosion, which should make even a novice thinker wonder, is it not true that wherever there is "matter" there must be "motion," and wherever there is motion there must be "time"? Therefore, staying with pure logic, the big bang must had happened after the accumulation of matter, which had to have existed prior to the big bang—the "point of singularity" that he and other alike scientist claim occurred in a billionth of a second. If this were the case, then matter must have been accompanied with both motion and time prior to the grand explosion. Again, it should be only logical to think that "time" existed before the big bang explosion and was not created during or a result of it.

Further in his book, writing about "the grand design," he claims that gravity was created from nothingness and was its own self-creator. To believe this is to believe that anything (or anybody) can make or give birth to itself. Why is gravity alone granted such unique powers if impersonal matter were floating around in space without hierarchy, form, or order? Is it not more plausible that it is Mr. Hawkins' personal bias against religion that has inspired him to take the role and presence of almighty creator our God and grant them to "almighty" gravity? He does not maintain the consistent logic that governs all science, starting with the laws of physics. In effect, these laws are like gynecologists, who simply deliver the baby from the "womb of mother nature," but they do not create the baby. Many other laws have been discovered using many reliable scientific theories, but in all of them the law of gravity operates without any exceptions.

It seems to me that Mr. Hawkins sees intelligent human beings as anthropoids, more resembling the apes, which are embroiled in their thought process and are confused and lost in their power of inference and accountability. He tosses such theoretical darts into the dark, hoping to score a bulleye that would help resolve his conundrum and riddling thoughts, but they convey too much ambiguity and hold no reason in the context of their delivery for anyone of sound mind to believe. Moreover, several prominent physicists claim that gravity is the weakest of the invisible forces by comparison. It flies in the face of reason that a scientist should be prejudicial instead of objective where such potent invisible forces of universe are not seen, and only their effect is known. It also seems suspect that, unlike many other notable scientists, Mr. Hawkins forgoes and ignores the effect of God's wonderful cosmic creation, our awesome universe with billions more universes that should put any competent mind at awe. Even setting aside the element of religion, but using pure logic, it simply makes no sense to believe that the inanimate force that is the law of gravity, with no mind, spirit, or soul, could be the cause and creator of all there is in this entire universe.

Mr. Hawkins and his cohorts need to consider logically, objectively, and without preconceived bias that there is only one cosmic energy that created and permeates everything there is. As they have been programmed by grand design (and not grand accident), each component must act its part in concert for a tranquil existence. They are only to be labeled and named differently the best we know how, and to avoid confusion and chaos, and to be able to identify and to exclusively designate the interactions and interdependencies of millions of entities, each of which plays its individual, vital role in our universe—including gravity. Nominating these forces of nature according to the vital task they perform does not mean they do run independently of other kinds of energy other than the originating energy of the entire cosmos. They were all here before us; all we have done is observe, name, and try to understand how they work. We did not create them any more than any individual part created all the others.

We utilize these consensual terminologies to be able to identify what we are blessed with and to make life easier and more practical, and the relatively simple role of the law of gravity is no exception. Further, it wouldn't be absurd to pose a simple, logical question to Mr. Hawkins about his published denial of God: "First, according to well-known physicists and modern astronomers, there are as many as planets and universes in this whole cosmos as there are sands on planet earth. Therefore—since we are living in and experiencing only one planet for a relatively short time, and because we possess finite and limited senses, not knowing much about the unseen world of subatomic and quantum reality, and since our senses do not have the frequency to vibrate fast enough to manifest the unseen world, and since it evidently requires other realm of existence to even detect such realities—shouldn't reasoning spur you a tad further not to conclude your findings just yet that an intelligent designer could not possibly be responsible for the origins of everything? A second question might be: Does not the world of science and reliable scientific methodology insist on knowing all of the significant variables in assessing their hypotheses, so that a correct and dependable finding could eventually materialize? In the same vein, how could it even be possible to reach a viable conclusion, if you, sir, and others have not factored in the unseen world (more accurately, will not)? Where what we can see even with the most advanced sophisticated telescopes is not all there is, yet the world of quantum mechanics, string theory, and many other complex entities continue to faithfully play their roles. Not only that, but the same entities are in many places at the same time. Who or what put all of this in place, including gravity, and who or what keeps everything coordinated? These are thoughts that have perplexed even the most intelligent of human minds, but the humble among them recognize the many things they do not know with certainty, including the origins of the universe and human life.

In this light, is it too much to ask if one is in need of better answers that they can stir up other exciting methods of inquiry to attract scientific investigation rather than inflating presumptuous findings based on personal bias that unscientifically repels logic with no deductive rationale. The point is that even when a phenomenon, an ideology, or any other entity believes it has completed its journey and reached its peak, there are always new thoughts that arise and often are compatible with or updates to prior beliefs, which may even be more in tune with the reality of our life and end up replacing the outdated ones. Religions are no exception, as the masses tend to interpret and decipher divine messages differently, which beliefs also travel through cultural and paradigm shifts and new, updated thoughts become undeniably real. These new transitional thoughts and mentalities should be respected, and contested with magnificent reasoning to prevent being misled. At the same time, one should be careful, as Spinoza says, to characterize God according to human behavior.

This should remind us of the Stone Age beliefs, when our predecessors thought someone stronger than them was causing all the occurrences and happenings that they did not comprehend. As the concept of God in various religions evolved, so did the fact that such subjects are controversial, extremely complex, and not everyone can digest the validity of these various transcendental messages. What was believed one, two, or ten thousand years ago and how it was applied simply will not be perceived the same as the contemporary age? In ancient times, ignorance, lack of information and knowledge, superstitions, dictatorial rulers, and so on, were ever present. Some slaughtered believers and others nonbelievers, or whomever did not comply with their insidious ways. The point is that there have always been many different beliefs, and each person ultimately is responsible for his or her own life and destiny. At the least, beliefs other than one's own should be respected, if not examined thoroughly to see if you might have missed something critical, but in no case should all religion be cast aside in a perfunctory, dismissive, and illogical manner such as Mr. Hawkins has done.

Meanwhile, I believe that we have at the least an infinite, intelligent, all-powerful energy that is ever-present regardless of who believes in its existence, which energy has orchestrated the universe so beautifully, and has so magnificently disciplined every element to be applicable to and supportive of human life. Regardless of individual concepts of God, I personally believe his messages come in various forms and types of revelations and in various subtle ways. I heard a viable suggestion that the God who created the universe and mankind is capable of communicating in ways that supersede human modes.

By extension then, could God actually have delivered revelation to his chosen ones, and embodied them with the potentiality and ability to activate those spiritual laws? I say yes, and I also say the same way he conveyed and revealed messages in an enlightening and surprising way to miraculous-minded scientists who invented the impossible. What we might have once thought to be miracles are now realities. Who is to say which ideas were purely human without divine input? Consider the "miraculous" minds of Einstein, Edison, Newton, Pasteur, Avicenna, Buddha, Galileo, and so many other prominent scientists, scholars, philosophers, and medical geniuses who have contributed so positively to the human race, and who have been credited with saving countless lives. To think, there may be even more gifted messengers of hope to come in the future. Yes, I believe God even reveals things to atheists, so that they inadvertently become positive instruments—people like Darwin, Marx, Engels, Mao, Lenin, and others. Even Mr. Hawkins, of whom I have been critical, has made many positive contributions, which I credit to divine inspiration that is outside of his awareness and belief system. Most controversial issues involving mankind's welfare go through transitions and evolutions, progressing through decades and centuries of constructive philosophical debates and scientific discussions. As Alexander Graham Bell famously said about all his failed experiments, "If it takes 999 attempts to achieve success, then all efforts were equally valuable."

I do not belief that it is far from reality to see many types of "chosen ones" who have proven themselves to be exemplary and having God-given talents with heavenly attributes. Yes, God accolades some people to lead and to become saviors, not only as spiritual and moral guides, but also in the gamut of diversified human endeavors and other crucial human fields. They are truly blessed with extraordinary intelligence; they are seers who see and are so enlighteningly talented because of their tremendous wealth of knowledge. And yes, in the same way, prophets were the chosen and the geniuses anointed with specific feelings or inspirations of revelation addressed to them in ways we cannot comprehend. The bigger point is they were there, in their time and culture, to guide and lead humanity from their particular eras of darkness and ignorance; they were true role models because their advice and guidance proved to be nothing short of miraculous.

They were superbly outstanding, torching the way through the midst of darkness and being the beacon of hope for human race. If ever the machinations and evils of a demonic era were upon us, exercising perhaps far worse atrocities than humanity has seen to date, we surely would pray and beg for a savior who was blessed with a revelation from God to rescue us from the clutches of evil with kindness and mercy. As has been aptly said of soldiers during wartime, "There are no atheists in foxholes."

Freedom and its Implications

Patrick Henry (May 29, 1736 to June 6, 1799) was a founding father, an orator, and a politician who led the movement of independence in Virginia in the 1770s. He is famous for having said, "Give me liberty, or give me death." How relevant this statement still is today and how crucial in many parts of the world where human dignity and hopes are being stomped on and trampled by mean and ugly spirited dictators. In my view, wanting to promote freedom as a global brand is a good task, but then it also might not help and could even backfire; in other words, liberty and democracy should be substantiated with good intention and money well spent.

Ideally, freedom ought to become a way of life wherever it is desperately needed, and it should be implemented with every constructive means available, but it definitely cannot continue to be exported via wars. If done through violence, even success makes a bitter experience for everyone, in turn making freedom lovers and the supporters of democracy targets of critique rather than being a proud and potent force for their good cause and a savior for the oppressed. In the meantime, however, perhaps it would be possible to stop the wicked villains from forcing tyrannical laws on helpless people where fear rules. As an old poem states, "nightingale sings sweetest at the darkest hours, telling us not to lose hope, but to give it our best." Striving for freedom and liberty is not an easy chore, especially when it is against ruthless rulers. Since the cause for which defenders of freedom are fighting is a "just cause," however, where human dignity and worthiness must be restored, no matter how stormy the sea crashing against them, they shall overcome.

Yes, the nature of the resistance is very challenging and perilous, which constantly reminds the freedom fighters to stay alert and be tactful. Ironically, war has a tendency to make proponents of evil even stronger; it has a way of actually maturing "up-risers" with a toughened mind and body. Doubling down on their evil plans, the advance of liberty inspires them to survive the roughest of terrain and living conditions. It causes them to appreciate the marvel of modern media, where the dastardly sacrifices they make are witnessed by the world, and which keeps them gratified and revitalized in their collective effort to propel and to be resolute in their vision, making it a reality. The bravery and heroism that people show in squaring off with the enemies of freedom can perhaps be beyond belief.

This axiomatic reality mitigates fears to the point where even death is welcomed, making the risking of lives common, opening the door for many to be willing to be sacrificed for valor, which propaganda is perpetuated until such vital deeds for the cause are accomplished. We must realize that such a worthy endeavor as liberty has an inverse implication, which subtly is addressed in mutual trust where morality and human virtues are to play a centrifugal force in everyday social interactions. We must keep in mind that the proponents of liberty have an inherent responsibility to act ethically with every intention to do good deeds at the same time they dispatch the evildoers. This dynamic ideally becomes prevalently applicable through incorporating education and civility of mind and manner to its saturation point, which effort will inspire higher levels of self-respect and conduct.

There should not be any excuses left for making jaw-dropping mistakes and instead, plans should be in place for tangible remedies and proper therapy for correction, especially for small-scale wrongs, misdemeanors, and misconduct. In this era, freedom is a predominant concept that, overall, the majority of nations seek and desire to have, especially in developing and dictatorial countries. Understanding the notion of liberty and freedom is one thing, but installing it is not an easy task; in reality, it is an inordinately complicated matter that should remind us all of the expression, "Be careful what you wish for." Freedom is a sacred word, and it must be crafted, realized, and practiced with the utmost care and intelligence. If mishandled or abused, it will impact us all with dismal and dire effects that will be felt individually and collectively.

To define the essence of the word freedom is to say that each of us is free to exercise what each of us wishes to do. To try to capture all that is implied with freedom involves our collective rational mind and wise, virtuous character that does not create or maintain liberty easily but values due diligence, positive work, perseverance, and the countless constructive ideas required to make it happen. We must realize that there is fine line between being free to do the right thing and being free to be a menace to society, and that with liberty comes responsibility.

If every individual takes the law into his or her own hands, there is no state of freedom; rather, there is anarchy, which is the absence of social law or a civilized state. In this direction lies the destruction of liberty; therefore, whenever we are tempted to take that path, we should subdue our lower nature and engage our higher nature because something higher than the individual is at stake. It is true that the consciousness and good will of people should collectively be incentivized in a decently free and brotherly nation. Remember in free countries we are on our own, and everyone is relatively free (within the laws) to do whatever each one wants—whether good or evil. But know that when you do good, when you leverage your education, talents, and skills in positive and productive ways, you become what the system was designed to support, and you find as a rule that there are healthy cultural and societal guidelines that contribute to a successful and prosperous life. Then, not only will you and those around you benefit greatly, but society and the system also benefit tremendously. Thus, an innovative, motivated individual should have the passion to take advantage of the boundless opportunities that are offered, which, if positively applied, can become extremely fruitful.

The system immediately recognizes a potentially talented mind and does not hesitate to promote and groom you into a productive member of society since you will be in high demand. You will be one of the individuals who tends to achieve financial prosperity. Because you are to be promoted and acknowledged as an entrepreneur or a successful businessperson, millions of others witness the success and set similar objectives and goals, which are the required building blocks that a capitalist system demands in a free and vigorous society. This easily describes a win-win situation since not only you but also the system and society can flourish when act in harmony.

We ought to be reminded if we do not realize the golden opportunities that liberty provides, we perhaps will lack the wisdom to act on them when the opportunities present themselves. And then, in a desperate moment and without thinking clearly, perhaps somehow we will be willing to act with negligence and perhaps do wrong or even become an instrument of malice. In this case, the system certainly wins, since you are certain to be punished harshly with huge fines and/or confinement, depending on the degree of your crime or wrongdoing. It is only fair to say that in a capitalist system, which promotes a classified society, there also must be those available to do menial and the most horrible jobs. Subtly categorized as "faceless people," these are the countless masses working unattractive jobs for a living, each of whom by default lives with an inferiority complex of some sort. They are never able to fulfill what they crave and wish for, which sometimes happens to be prolonged throughout their entire life.

We should bear in mind that when someone is in violation of a free society's legal and ethical codes, and is at odds with what it honors and stands for, the entire society of contributing taxpayers is negatively affected. We must be careful to acquire education, skill, and a vocation that is professionally in high demand, and also is prestigious enough to earn a good life. Whatever you must do, you must not allow yourself to become an outcast for any reason, no matter the excuse, because such a society can be incredibly unforgiving. On the other hand, this is a system that has the ability to bring you goodness and treasures on a silver platter, if only you have been **awakened** and can be seen as a good candidate to serve society's purposes.

Remember that the system always wins no matter if any one individual loses or thrives and wins; thus, the culprit who does wrong, perhaps just by not being forthright and righteous, will carry the burden and pay a heavy price if penalized and convicted of a crime. It is of huge importance not to become arrogant and lured into believing that it is a free country and you perhaps can do whatever you wish. Whenever someone does wrong, society is negatively impacted, and the wrongdoers can fully expect to be punished accordingly—theoretically, with due process of the law, but even that is not always guaranteed once you end up on the wrong side of justice. But the system wins regardless.

Of course, it would be desirable if the system could figure out how to self-correct in productive ways to halt crime through education and meaningful training, rather than being so one-track minded financially as to be willfully blind and stoic about such destructive parts of its own system. When any system is adamant to create and maintain a free society, and such freedom is to be fully unleashed because it is in such high demand, then there must be countless professional counselors, competent social workers, and quality social services to help those in need of mental and behavioral guidance to operate productively in a civilized and rational minded society to lessen rampant felony crimes and criminals.

Let me be explicit there is no ambiguity about freedom and you must acquire the required level of education and valued training, along with an emphasis on mental and spiritual development, which go hand-in-hand. Priority must be given for all types of manufacturing, blue collar, and other service-oriented people, who earnestly believe in being true and honest human beings with good character. If society cannot accommodate those who comprise the majority of its own support network, then rest assured their beastly side sooner or later will prevail and devastate the minority who govern and otherwise normally control such destructive elements of society. When we are free we are able to follow our dreams, and this gives everyone a chance to work hard for self-efficacy and success, which happens naturally when people are free to follow their passion in a system that makes such pursuit of passion possible. They become self-energized, creative, and innovative, since a pleasant atmosphere and an encouraging environment exempt from discriminatory factors or bias is conducive to their success.

Yes, you who are dreamers should dream big, because you are free to reach stars, and you can know that even when you fail at first, your desire and perseverance acts like a premium jet fuel, propelling you forward and making you stronger, which gives you rocket like momentous to reach and to objectify your goal. It is only fair to say that no system can come close to promoting individual freedom better than the proponents of our system of democracy and freedom. In spite of the many flaws and imperfections, this is still the best option presently available. Of course, one hopes that it will further mature so that it pays more attention to human rights, with more equity in the allocation of resources, and also upgrades and makes education more prevalent and available. These and other positive investments will help to suppress unrestrained violence, and then perhaps ever increasing tax funds could be better spent in productive and preventive ways rather than spending it after problems ignite and become inflamed, in policing, incarceration, capital punishment, and other fire control methods that only treat symptoms when things are already out of control.

I would also encourage people to look at the long and arduous waiting lines of newcomers to every western country's consulate asking for a visa, and in particular the U.S.; all of them wanting to flee their own ruined society and join one of the free nations of the world. Because freedom is an undeniable, natural, and crucial component of the human spirit, when it is denied, one begins the slow and terrible suffocation of the spirit of life itself. At the same time, of course we have room for improvement, and we must improve since there are many glaring flaws within the system, but we must never forget that in spite of all the needed improvements, there is also more hope and flexibility for progress and positive change in this system than any other system known to man.

We ought to remember this great statement from John Stuart Mill, who said, "If mankind minus one were of one opinion, mankind would be no more justified in silencing that one person than if he had the power, would he be justified in silencing mankind." Freedom and democracy should be available universally to all mankind; as the rain and the sun do not differentiate among people, neither should we let others to suffer under cruel and inhumane forms of government.

We can truly understand these realities only when we experience friendship across cultures and realize that there are many good people in all communities; people with compassionate hearts and profound wisdom. Especially in our modern world, we have access to virtually all the world's communities. Since technology has made reaching one another quite doable even in the most of remote places, we should be about reaching across and building bridges so that we might enlighten each other and **wake each other up**. Nelson Mandela said, "It is not our diversity which divides us; it is not our ethnicity, or religion or culture that divides us. Since we have achieved our freedom, there can only be one division amongst us: between those who cherish democracy and those who do not."

What if the Afterlife was a Certainty and not a Mystery?

If we were sure about life after death, we would not be so fearful of dying as are do now; in fact we would not hesitate to jump into our death, especially if we knew we were going to land or appear in a better place than the one we are experiencing. What would happen if we were absolutely certain of the message from the afterlife and if we truly believed what is said in holy books and by prophets about the afterlife?

Imagine a world where we know the promises of the afterlife are authenticated and a sure thing—that one's decent character and good deeds are noted and assured to be recompensed: with milk and honey, streams of crystal clear water, artesian wells, magical oases, plenty of one's favorite foods, such as exotic fruits, assorted nuts and sweets, and a wealth of incredible entertainment options. Boredom utterly could not exist in the afterlife, with its unlimited varieties of rich gardens beyond human imagination, distinguished birds of paradise, and vibrant trees providing a refreshing and sensuous atmosphere. A paradise where beautiful and domesticated animals roam across deep, luscious green and fertile ground, spotted with breathtakingly colorful flowers and eye-catching bees and butterflies.

Along with all of the above luxuries, imagine the males among us having plenty of gorgeous and intoxicating angel-like "females" available for our pleasure at all hours, and an over-supply of handsome "males" for females to be with, ready to serve and relax them. Astonishing singers and sensational musicians wander, playing one's favorite music. Imagine a life far away from what has cluttered our collective mind and spirit, a life where financial burden, family violence, crime beyond belief, greed, jealousy, death of loved ones, and thousands of other ills, could not occur. We are depleted of disease and chronic sickness, and likewise experience no stress, depression, impact from war, bad accidents, or terrorism. There is no global warming and no overeating of toxic foods filled with GMOS (genetically modified organisms), bringing us closer to death. Imagine having no mundane violence of any kind—neither religious- nor state-inspired terrorism—and no domesticated warfare. Pain and suffering would become things of the past, with no meaning and perhaps even not known or felt by anyone.

In the afterlife, LOVE would be truly applicable and sacredly exercised. Can you imagine a place where all of your dreams can come true? A place where abundance, joy, beauty, love, compassion, truth, art, transcendence, and all other dignified states of being are manifested? Where justice and peace effortlessly prevail, and no mystery or ambiguity can distract our minds with thoughts about the uncertainties of the afterlife? In such a scenario, the afterlife is known to be truth—a genuine and heavenly gift—and not just a presumption.

Finally, envision a place where selfishness and cynicism would not be tolerated, and one's demonic behavior and wicked actions are destined to be dealt with stringently. Since rogue and mischievous attitudes and bad personalities would be considered wrong and unjustified, they would no doubt be severely punished. As inadvertent mistakes would be quickly identified and forgiven; then what do we sincerely think could happen?

I believe then that we would act in good faith and not in breach of our commitment to the welfare of society. Hence we would behave with virtue and dignity, effectively deterred from moral turpitude. We would behave decently knowing the end results are real; if we do not operate with goodness in heart, mind, and spirit, such acts are not redeemable and therefore are horrifyingly punishable. In addition, the chance of not getting caught would not exist and escaping consequence is out of the question. We know we are being monitored by an omnipresent God, who is beyond our reach in time and space. A relative piece of heaven where we individually belong can become practical, and we will assuredly enjoy the afterlife.

A second alternative is also a sure thing, which is to "commit suicide." When one is having an arduous and challenging time that ultimately escalates to a prolonged, gradual and torturous life, he or she may decide to steer away from having to deal with pain and suffering of this world. Such a life causes one to feel and act stir-crazy and distraught. One then meditates on leaving for another domain where being well-nurtured is promised and he or she can sustain all of the amenities of glamorous living that will certainly materialize in the afterlife. To escape to a life that is fulfilling and free from any kind of anxieties of the mundane world provides a good opportunity for one to exit at one's discretion any time one feels like it. For these individuals it is an almost impossible task to stay and live here on planet earth where it seems to be a harsh and mandatory test for us humans—especially knowing there is another realm of existence that offers authentic happiness and delight.

It is noteworthy to know that we would still make mistakes, even if the afterlife is not postulated but empirically known to be fact. Being human means that we have not only good intentions, but are also impacted by vile and bad feelings and resentment, which we can act upon. But then, our deliberate evil conduct and intent to cause harm should be dramatically diminished, unless one is naively insane. I am sure we have all heard the cliché "knowledge is power." The irony is that if we understand the afterlife, then the knowledge will surely backfire, becoming an easy ticket to our being doomed and not wanting to be here, even if for a relatively short time. Imagine if each of us was placed in infinite universes according to our actions and moral standards. It is scientifically claimed that there are more universes in the cosmos than the amount of refined sands on our planet earth. If so, each and every person could be accommodated and positioned where one belonged.

I am sure we would be on our best behavior in order to receive our heavenly rewards after we expire, or else clearly be motivated to leave for celestial realms, not wanting to bear the pressures and hardships of our life here on planet earth. The point is: there is a reason for this whole universe. If the afterlife were not so mysterious, our world could not be sustained. To reach where one is destined to go requires an individual to perhaps experience a phase that must be endured before the next phase, if any, can be fulfilled. Otherwise there would clearly be no life the way we know it and as it is devised, we would be bound to destruction. Bertrand Russell puts it this way: "the whole problem with the world is that fools and fanatics are always so certain of themselves, and wiser people so full of doubt." Francis Bacon said, "If a man will begin with certainties, he shall end in doubts; but if he will be content to begin with doubts, he shall end in certainties." But what Krishnamurti said about death is perhaps closest to reality. "Death is extraordinarily like life when we know how to live. You cannot live without dying. You cannot live if you do not die psychologically every minute. This is not an intellectual paradox. To live completely, wholly, every day as if it were a new loveliness, there must be a dying to everything of yesterday, otherwise you live mechanically, and a mechanical mind can never know what love is or what freedom is."

What is Wrong?

There is an answer. It is time for us to reject the version of God that corporate religions are insisting we believe in. This "God" is used by corporate religion to maximize profit in his name and institutionalize faith, as well as to embolden the unbelievers and agnostics in their hypocritical behavior. A truly loving God needs no bribe to know we exist, and identifies with a child of the Almighty who is in bondage and in pain. There are so many wrongdoers who have lost touch with the reality of our creator and with what the essence of humanity should be; these individuals have effectively turned into vultures.

Corporate religion is responsible for most of the ill wills of the world and remains the cause of many demonic social, political, and economic outcomes. A miserable life is being bitterly experienced by billions of innocent people who literally have no way out of their dire situation. They are treacherously hapless, helpless, and hopeless. How can anyone in his right mind and spirit honestly think it is appropriate to chop someone's arm off for taking a loaf of bread, while the real thieves plunder all there is in the name of God and are protected by law? This makes fair allocation of resources a farce and a comical behavior. Lysander Spooner said, "Those who are capable of tyranny are capable of perjury to sustain it." People currently staying quiet about such travesty of thought and action need to alert humanity of the culture of fear prevalent in such atmospheres.

Is it unclear to most people that no matter how resilient a free market economy is to be, it is always going to have accompanied with it some degree of unemployment and inflation and so on. This is where social subsidies and welfare should be strictly controlled and managed to reach those devastatingly helpless people that are the victims of unemployment and its offshoots in such a system. Such individuals risk their limbs being cut off in order to provide food for their mostly sick and destitute families, just because they are desperate and cannot find jobs. Any fool ought to know that such inhumane punishments are meant to inject fear into society and serve to uphold the power of their own cruel and inefficient governing state, and are certainly not required by a loving God.

Can anyone claiming decency not find these fiendish attributes disgusting? And what should one do when stuck between a rock and a hard place—either not provided with a decent job to make a living, or hit with capital punishment, becoming the victim of such abhorrent policies and incompetency of the system? We must realize that a sick economy will induce a sick environment, making ours a cutthroat society. If real thieves are allowed leverage to appropriate what belongs to people, it is surely not going to help at all.

Always know who you are dealing with. As Warren Buffet said, "You cannot make a good deal with a bad person." I bet if you put people with integrity, righteousness in deed, and ethically fitted character in charge of what we know as free market economy, it should work fine, and with minimal casualties. A fair competition must be allowed to prevail within the market mechanism, where the efficiency of the market itself is not doubted, only those avarices replacing the invisible hand of the market.

Nietzsche (1844-1900) believed many higher cultures were formed on the basis of cruelty and force, and were unjustly shaped to serve those in a position of power and the elites.

One should think twice about believing otherwise, since the veracity of such a claim is so finely textured, making it difficult to detect with a naked eye the everyday violation of people's rights. There are those who are neglected who have no face; they are barely noticed when they are in pain and suffering. And yes, they are the ones who innocently bear the burdens of bad social, political, and economical decision-makings of big institutions—where sinners get away scot-free and the poor are left holding bags of calamities, where their cries are lost in bureaucracy and red tape. What we seem to be numb to and cannot decode is this fact of "what goes around comes around." When the culprits face punishment by the cosmos, they are dumb enough not to be able to connect the crime they perpetrated with the sentenced punishment. That is sad beyond belief.

We are all connected, much like a drop from the ocean that cannot survive if not preserved as part of the ocean. There is a natural order to this intricately designed world, which if defied, will eventually bring nothing short of destruction. Any centrifugal force or deliberate attempt away from what is intelligently devised will be bound to fail. We are to establish our position within the world by doing well and what is destined, understanding that we are purposefully directed to reach these objectives. We must habituate our conduct accordingly. The same idea applies to those who live a luxurious life in an upscale environment where they play a key role in controlling the economy and other vital sources of society's interactions. It is difficult to understand that a top-down government needs to be in close vicinity to its people's depravity and helplessness, where there exists a desperate fight to preserve a very basic living standard.

Unless government officials experience people's pain and suffering; how on heaven and earth would it be possible to know what they actually feel and are going through? It is simply not possible. Perhaps if down-top government were not applicable it would be worse than what it is, since most likely we would need to deal with lack of literacy and education of authorities and other parties involved. If knowledge and wisdom is absent, autocracy and dictatorship of some sort is bound prevail, therefore again the way to relative prosperity for all is to "live and to let live."

This should make sense to those with a good conscience who are integrated with morality in spirit and civility of thought and manner; it will not make sense to those estranged by having none. How could any nation tolerate a government that hides behind the veil of religion, and in its name causes so many vile and abhorrent acts? Does moral righteousness and goodness not identify with religious, spiritual and Godly conduct? If it does, how could it ever be possible for politics to mix with divine law when it is the nature of politics to breed dubious behaviors and sometimes vicious maneuvers, and to perpetuate covert actions filled with top secret information and lies in order to survive?

Why should God and religion be anyone's exclusive territory, or any government or institution's right to rule over people, dictating to them the way of life and how they should live it? These are nothing more than schemes manufactured by politicians to secure their own affluent living, camouflaged by associating the almighty God with fear, effectively bludgeoning people in his name.

Why would any entity in good conscience want to meddle with the most private and sacred of beliefs—that in the divine—where people seek refuge in their most desperate of times, asking God for replenishment of their soul and spirit and for forgiveness and mercy? When is this obtrusiveness, perpetrated by those in control and representing ill vigilance, going to halt for good? It is the twenty- first century; there is no need for such fraudulent activities that surely contradict people's awakening consciousness and their chosen life style.

Uncalled-for Conditioning

Our prefrontal cortex plays a very significant role in perceiving the difference between right and wrong. Neuroscience has shown that a young person's cognitive development carries on into his or her later stages in life. Intellect and wisdom, judgment, decision-making, emotional maturity and self-image are malleable until the prefrontal cortex of the brain has fully developed. The medical community believes that our prefrontal cortex matures at roughly twenty-five to thirty-five years of age. It shouldn't be surprising then, that many under the designated age of maturity for the prefrontal cortex have a difficult time wisely deciding between what is right and what is wrong, especially if some of their challenges involve abstract programming's that are difficult to deal with. This can put many adolescents, teens, and young adults at risk and vulnerable to misconduct and destructive behaviors.

Understanding that the development of different regions of the brain is not concurrent helps us to see the concept of adolescent risk-taking in a whole new light. What we should also pay attention to is the fact that our subconscious mind, which is on autopilot at all times, is synchronized with and grasps events taking place in our life. Therefore when so much violence and sex is shown in the mainstream media via movies, TV, news, and other home entertainment sources (internet, magazines, and so on), our sub-conscious is bound to pick most of it up as real since it cannot tell the difference between fact and fiction.

It exacerbates the situation when many individuals are perhaps not conscious or intelligent enough to realize that the culture of violence encouraged by the entertainment industry exists to make money. Huge financial cartels and holding companies are working very hard to maximize their profits, regardless of what types of messages these amusements give, and who the victims are.

It gets even worse in places where wisdom and the average level of knowledge is below the expected range. When people are not able to employ functional analytical skills, it is sometimes very difficult to make sense of intricate conditionings, which are subtly managed and prone to make troubles. It is sad but true that we are being conditionally shaped and patterned, and yes, we do contest mental molding and filter what we seem not to be interested in; our thoughts and conscious mind constantly challenge these ubiquitous learnings to prevent being pixilated (odd in behavior). But then, part of this culture of conditioning includes the subliminal use of research-oriented programs, cleverly infused into our thought processes. Such programming makes it likely that the information presented will be grasped by our subconscious mind, resulting in a weak chance for effective retaliation. That is perhaps why, if anyone thinks and chooses to maneuver out of what is known as norms, they will be labeled rebellious and out of guild.

The point is, why do we act and behave the way we do? Is this what is left of humanity? Are we really condemned to criteria that have exhausted our hopes and efforts, making us act indifferent and numb towards finding meaningful solutions for a better life? Yes, it is challenging to overcome what we are fed so constantly since our mind believes what we feel, see, hear, taste, and smell. If we are not contemplating and searching for guidance out of these mental conditioning traps, we will surely be victims, for doing things habitually and not noticing what is to us customary is exactly what we have been addicted to and shaped for. Remember: repetition brings habit. Sometimes when exposed to information routinely, thoughts are formed so callously that they are then literally taken as reality, no matter how damaging. Deepak Chopra said, "What gets in our way is history and culture and religion and economic conditions. It is part of the hypnosis of our social conditioning."

I believe we behave as we are programmed, without actually mulling over our actions and realizing them. This can sometimes create enormous pain and suffering for ourselves and others because the dimension of our awareness is not raised, and cannot fully grasp decisive and significant matters. Such awareness, or lack thereof, can probably denote the difference between a happy life and our demise. Krishnamurti stated, "It is no measure of health to be well-adjusted to a profoundly sick society."

Our being a menace to self, people around us and others can sometimes make it difficult to see the silver lining, especially if one is conditionally patterned, or if one's own deeper thoughts have no maturity and heightened intelligent. Is it nature or nurture that is responsible for our wrongdoing and/or for our good behavior and success? The solution is to constantly raise our awareness and not become the victim of such imposed circumstances as "conditional patterns," until such an atmosphere weakens and collapses. To conquer the unconscious harmful behaviors means replacing them with an educated and alert mind. We must modulate our conduct and not give in to any type of molded thinking, which is aimed at controlling us rather than being controlled by us. It is a known reality that our good and bad thoughts do steadfastly wrestle, and yet our deep thoughts can win by controlling our ego and refusing to become enslaved. We ought to seek true freedom, which means not falling for what is manufactured and fake. General Henri Frederic Amiel, Swiss educator and philosopher (1795-1881) said, "We become actors without realizing it, and actors without wanting to."

We need to understand while we are in a waiting mode that we will always be in a waiting mode. We should live in the present and enjoy the little things in life. We should find peace of mind, and as we should feel the goodness of life, and feel the intensity of being alive. We ought to break free from those things to which we are subjectively conditioned (influenced mainly by sex, money, power, and other peripherally related incentives) to allow the fulfillment of the promise of greater happiness that the future is to bring us.

Not living our present moment fully, hence leaving what we can be happy with in a waiting mode, means that perhaps our wishes will never be fulfilled. Imagine that someone that you dearly wish for and are practically obsessed with comes into your life and then leaves you. Be cautious of what you wish for, since what makes one happy can also spell disaster. Money is what is most desired and sought for, however being incredibly rich and wealthy, but then not wise, can definitely lead to a dismal outcome.

It is of utmost importance to pay attention to the rivalry between what makes sense and is freedom-based (not anxiety-driven), and what is meant to enslave us, no matter how potently we desire it, or the material importance attached. When one enters any addictive mode, it is as though one starts by hitting the finger with a sledgehammer, repeating the assault until eventually the hammer strikes the skull. We need to constantly seek constructive new ways to free ourselves from the bondage of tradition and ill cultural ways that have wrongly affected us. Krishnamurti alleged, "Tradition becomes our security, and when the mind is secure it is in decay." I believe we are complacently addicted to our way of life; our culture has denied us the truth and in this, we are unknowing in how to truly live.

Stephen R. Covey points out in his *7 Habits of Highly Effective People*: "The reflection of the current social paradigm tells us we are largely determined by conditioning and conditions." Because addiction leaves people with a compulsive psychological need, it is colossally difficult to quit. And if one does not have the resources to be assisted in these efforts, then it is a sure bet that the final below to the head will be administered. Since we are surrounded with a culture of "red alert" conditioning, if we are not cautious and enlightened, we will find ourselves subjugated and ultimately harmed by it. Our culture encourages us to become habitually enslaved to money, power, drugs, gambling, alcohol, hoarding, lying, sex and pedophilia, overeating and literally thousands of other culprits that can threaten to put human life at a high risk of annihilation. Come to think of it, most of these uncalled-for behaviors are motivated and become further hypertrophied through the billions—if not trillions—of dollars spent incentivizing them. Imagine then, the colossal monetary return!

What Should be Done?

What is it that keeps humanity from tasting life in its entire heavenly offering, instead reducing it to ashes for the majority of human beings? Why is it that despite billions of years of experience and readily available information about our past and our difficult journey to the present, we are still carrying tons of baggage of ignorance and unawareness?

We have faced the same problem over and over again—not realizing that humans should not be trusted with too much power. Power has been proven to have consistently evil repercussions. People with too much power breathe in a higher ground. When a powerful king or queen with an enormous empire and government attacks others' sovereignty, is not because they have no food, clothing, shelter, or women. They commit such atrocities because of unrestrained ambition, wanting to prove their insane power even further. John Steward Mill said, "Human natural tendency is to impose their way on others, this advocacy is so strong that only the depletion of power can halt it." If preventive measures are not taken to deter these bullies, then their dominance and dictatorial behavior will force others to obey without question; diversity in thought-provoking ideas, different opinions and open mindedness are punished and choked upon inception. Such abuse of power eventually leads to a peasant-like society where people are compelled into becoming quiet and lamb-like in nature, in complete surrender to fascism. Berlin Isaiah said, "Too much power is a danger lurking to hunt freedom." Amy Goodman said, "We need a media that covers power, not covers FOR power." The average intelligence is still raw and unripe; we keep making the same mistake that throws us backward, and reminds us of the stone ages.

We ought to understand that the twenty-first century is an era where attitudes like inferiority complexes and superiority complexes are rampant. These and other human malaise enslave us, sometimes to a point of no return. No one should be trusted with too much of anything, especially when it comes to power.

We need to stop pussyfooting around and evading this very problem that has yoked humanity with dire effects for so long in many parts of the world, crushing people's spirit for true democracy. It seems our cortex, the part of the human brain that controls our thoughts and emotions, just goes haywire—and is conquered when it comes to having the absolute might it needs to be rebuked and stopped. The euphoria of power is akin to elation, but also makes one addicted to being feared. Being feared in turn leads to isolation from the rest of society, since normal social interaction cannot occur based on threat. If such totalitarian power is to be maintained, eventually one must seek refuge in dictatorship and fascism.

Why should we blame anything other than our lack of knowledge and understanding of an issue that has been hurting us for so long? People like Walter Lippmann were successful in analyzing our attention deficit disorder. He believed that: "a system of elite should rule the rest of us, as we are not able of being rational in our decision makings, and the end result could be disastrous if left alone." That might be true to some extent, but still, you put anyone person, or any one group of elite in a position of absolute power (including Mr. Lippmann or Mr. Edward Barany, from the same school of thought), and trust me: they will turn into a "bad lemon" and will show the same undesirable effect of corruption. We are to learn and put into practice the theory that no one, no group of elite, and no network of any kind should be allowed too much might and power. Because if it happens, then Mr. Lippmann and Mr. Barany's are right in addressing "rationality" to that effect. Part of the problem is that not enough resources and capital are spent on education and training, which could empower people to make resourceful and rational decisions, by utilizing wisdom and a good sense of judgment.

We need to learn not to be mesmerized in our decision and vote, and not to bestow unwarranted accolades upon the throne of the kingdom, even if we are forced. If Socrates, Plato, or Aristotle were alive, they would offer us the philosopher king. I believe this is possible, much like we currently produce experts in neurology, sophisticated and trustworthy brain and heart surgeons, dynamic psychologists, expert astronauts, and so on. We must make a collective effort toward putting an end to allowing anyone to hold absolute power. If we do not, we will place the lives of millions at risk. George Orwell said, in 1984, "We know no one ever seized power with the intention of relinquishing it."

We should select righteous people with no tendency toward moral turpitude, and train them as watch dogs to oversee emergent character flaws in ruling parties, no matter what kind of governance is in place. I also believe these indoctrinated human watchdogs must be accommodated with a balance of reasonable wealth and comfort so that financial deprivation could not become a motive for them to lose their integrity and to be bought and bribed. This role should also be fortified and backed up with punishment should it lead to betrayal, resuming the pragmatic nature of punishment and reward. Have you not paid attention to the corporate powers as they are unleashed with no muzzle? Should we not learn from our history that empires permitted to grow gigantic are propelled to fall, sometimes in a dangerously accelerated fashion? Just consider the lessons learned from others before us. When are we going to take notice of this attention deficit disorder strangling us with the intention to kill? It is time for these huge financial powers to wake up and smell the coffee—to realize that they can only go so far before being negatively affected by their very own mistakes. This logic might seem invisible, however since we—God, nature, and ourselves—are all interconnected, be assured that this inevitability is not a mirage.

Do not let the accumulation of wealth and so much power get into your head, blocking your vital decision to make a difference and to bring out the best in people instead of the worst. Doing so is sure to lead to a no-win situation. History can attest to many instances that world leaders who make war tend to have a particular personality profile, specifically a high need for power. American presidents who exhibit this need have, throughout history, been more likely to take their country into war than those who don't. Dwight Eisenhower didn't show it for instance, while George W. Bush did. This "need for power" was identified by the great psychologist David McClelland as one of three basic, largely unconscious drives, which motivate people to different degrees.

The need for power (the other needs are for affiliation and achievement) is where you are motivated to dominate and control what other people want, need or fear. In simulations of the Cuban missile crisis, where nuclear holocaust between Russia and USA was narrowly averted, people who score high in terms of their need for power played the role of war room decision makers. They tended to take actions which would have, in 1962, led to war. All leaders need to have a certain appetite for power; leadership is too stressful otherwise, and power's effects on the brain acts as a sort of anti-depressant. But like all addictive drugs, too much for too long of using drugs, causes dangerous changes in the brain, which include reckless disinhibiting, risk-blindness and difficulty in seeing things from other's perspectives. Ex-UK Foreign Secretary Lord Owen has described this condition as the "Hubris Syndrome," which he diagnosed leaders Margaret Thatcher, Tony Blair and George W Bush, among others, as showing. Few if any leaders can survive more than ten years of power without being tipped into this dangerous state of altered personality and increased desire for even more power.

Most democracies have devised constraints—limited terms of office for instance—to counteract such dangerous changes to the brain. It is the neurologically-created conceit of many powerful leaders that, in the words of Louis XV of France, "après moi le deluge" (after me, the flood). Power fosters the delusion of indispensability. Many political leaders have created havoc by fighting to stay in their post because they genuinely believe their abilities are crucial for the survival of their country and that no-one else can do it. Vladimir Putin has held power in Russia as president or prime minister for approaching 15 years, too long for any one man or woman's brain to endure without dangerous changes that foster recklessness and a blindness to other perspectives. American author and essayist Edward Abbey said, "Power is always dangerous. Power attracts the worst and corrupts the best."

Putin's military incursion into Ukraine may be a particularly worrying symptom of his affliction. I believe we have reached an age, through the maturity of our consciousness and deeds, in which we should be aware and weary of the hazardous and horrendous implications of too much power. We should understand that this imbalance leaves behind irreparable damages, and needs to be watched closely and stopped where it is either forced or active. William E Channing said, "Absolute power was not meant for man." It is just unfortunate that too much power can lure man into behaving his worst, and is so addictive that it becomes the ultimate aphrodisiac stemming from human nature.

It is a vital task to collectively bargain for funding to be used toward positively educating the masses. Upgrading the public's knowledge of social, cultural, political and financial sciences and awareness is key. It is in turn critical to impart appropriate decision making skills, so that turning too much power over to anyone or to any entity can be avoided. Retributions are exponentially damaging when mistakes are made; literacy and knowledge is the only hope left for good citizens to learn and to understand this intricate world and its faculties, ultimately distinguishing them from quacks.

Do Not Get Duped (Bamboozled)

When judging another's character by seeing, hearing, and/or thinking about them, we can be tricked into believing that what we think we know about them should somehow manifest as factual. This could not be any further from the truth, since many individuals artistically play perplex roles, and are sometimes the product of complex environments. There is a lot more to one's character than meets the eye. It is when we are not able to see through some devious soul, premeditating to cause us harm, which is then, when we become off guarded and a victim of our own wrong decision, since we naively trusted them, and hence taken for a fool. As our world is getting ever smaller, and cross-cultural integration is an inevitable fact, we are bound to run into these con artists, and may be deceived. This deception could come with a heavy price.

It is of grave importance to be keen, and patience is a "must" to subtly evaluate these hoodlums since some of them have sneaky characters and ill intended minds. When so it happens that such individuals are situated in the mainstream of a sophisticated civilization, it becomes a game-changer. Because they have not naturally evolved with the system and are not attuned to it (hence not informed enough or enlightened), in which some of them cause irreparable damages through growth negligent.

People which are devoid of educational opportunities, and have not yet learned the morale of the system in which they operate can act irresponsible, and sometimes behave no less than a beast, behaving irrationally and destroying all that is in their path—just like a rhino that is depleted of any common sense. What these nomads are equipped with, however, is the ability to emotionally prey on philanthropists and trusting people. And if they eventually climb to the top of the ladder, they inject deadly venom into the very people who helped them without any shame or remorse, giving meaning to the old adage "no good deed goes unpunished." This leaves behind an ugly consequence with rather a nervous soul to think twice before helping again. Once a good Samaritan has been bitten or screwed over once or twice (or has witnessed similar ill experiences first-hand) the hurt and bitter experiences make him dubious and uncertain if he should help or not. The resulting lack of trust should remind anyone of this rule of thumb that needs to be honed: "if it sounds too good to be true, it probably is."

Trust your intuition and listen to your gut feeling. One should take a second and a third look, and meditate on one's trending thoughts, language, and conduct; this should help detect or avoid the deception. Be wary of some of these characters with a predator-like mentality, who act from pure instinct like animals. Many with such predatory personalities have additional factors that contribute to their overall ill will: lack of education, financial depravity, mental and physical insecurities, lack of proper role models, sexual or emotional abuse, or these individuals may have been abused as children, brought up in a culture of fear and security and constantly preyed upon,

Whether a victim of imposition and bad circumstances or by choice, a threat is a threat until constructively restored with decent behavior, cognitive training and education. Benjamin Franklin said, "Tricks and treachery are the practice of fools, that don't have brains enough to be honest." And Richard Shea said in The Book of Success quote: "You can win by fraud and deceit, but evil leaves an itch you can't scratch."

Naïve people whom do not value democracy, know it is a free society and wrongly think they have free reign to unleash filth, profanity, and sadistic thoughts and ideas—and can do as they wish, since it is protected under the freedom of speech and freedom of the press (and many other miracle-like laws and opportunities given to the masses by the good old Constitution). What they forget is that they should not infringe upon other's rights in their actions, nor should they violate sovereignty. These individuals are unduly mistaking freedom and civility of mind and manner for the right to engage in inappropriate behaviors, therefore resulting in untamed and unrestrained attitude. They use their street smarts to leverage emotional favor with vulnerable people to get what they have carefully orchestrated for. These types of social outcome and interactions should remind us of Shakespeare, who says: "True justice, and a just world is hard to implement," reminding us of a theatre-like world, where its actors and actresses are impersonators, finely playing their starring role.

It would be a blessing in disguise if and only if these actions could perhaps makes us wiser, and concurrently assist society in gaining reliable experience. Therefore we should be alerted not to make judgment on what we see or hear, but to meditate deeper and not get entangled by the emotional bondage. We must have patience and study who we are dealing with, since mistakes can sometimes be extremely costly, especially after a point of no return. This is not to say that compassion and goodness should, God forbid, ever be bypassed; it is simply to say we need to be cautious and realize to whom our kindness is rendered.

Try to notice elusive behaviors. If you are sharp and have a curious nature even the detection of an incorrectly uttered word could probably signal a red light from these undesirable deceivers of society. One must not become delusional or unable to distinguish fact from fiction, when it comes to what is to be allocated to righteous people. It is necessary to forego those with wrong attributes, since if they ever become strengthened and supported in their malicious intent, innocent people in their path can get critically hurt. As Plato says, "goodness is its own virtue."

We should always practice kindness as we are exercising caution, and should not get punished because of it. If you are cheated once, then you should be adamant in addressing the wrongdoers, stating that "I am a good person and I will forgive you, but rest assured I am not out of my mind, and would be obtuse to ever trust you again. I shouldn't have trusted you more than you deserved." Abraham Lincoln said, "You can fool all the people some of the time, and some of the people all the time, but you cannot fool all the people all the time."

Reaching Stars

What is it that motivates and pushes some to relentlessly pursue their dreams, no matter how many times they fall? They rise with due diligence and carry on, making a strong commitment to their exclusive task, where relentlessly persevere to challenge the most difficult of circumstances. It seems they have thoroughly understood what Confucius reminded us, when he said: "The will to win, the desire to succeed, the urge to reach your full potential ... these are the keys that will unlock the door to personal excellence." Motivated individuals are programmed to reach for and conquer what they are focused on with a one-track mind. It looks like they repeatedly place themselves where they have aimed, believing themselves to be practically there, n imagining and glorifying their cause further every step of the way. This amplifies their efforts even more, making them as aggressively excited as truly reaching their goal, which in turn propels them ever closer to the winning finish line with no hesitancy at all.

It seems they are estranged for having the slightest clue of impossibility or any hindrance in reaching their goal, or even thinking of being reluctant. This should remind us of Eleanor Roosevelt, who said, "with the new day comes new strength and new thoughts." Their resoluteness and obsession with what they want and aspire for makes them immune and impervious to all sorts of hardship, mistakes and the hurdles confronting them. Their resiliency and efforts should remind the rest of us of myth and methodology suited best to ancient heroes.

Ancient heroes—fighting against the most vicious and horrifying villains, overcoming the invincibility of the culprits embodied and told of in allegories. The stories of their successes make them legends that enlighten and encourage the rest of us as we see them as symbols of resistance. Victorious against all odds, giving hope and encouragement to the rest by making us believe that there is always a light at the end of the tunnel. We hope to follow in their footsteps so that perhaps one day we too become super stars, or at a minimum, learn a valuable lesson about not quitting easily and continuing to reach for our dreams when faced with uncertainties and troubles. Walt Disney puts it this way, "if you can dream it, you can do it." One thing is for sure: these legends and shining stars did not fall from the sky and other planets, nor are they some sort of extraterrestrial species. No, they are here among us. What makes them different and extraordinarily successful it that they have figured out and discovered what they are good at, and what they love to do.

These individuals are then able to zealously manipulate their talent and with persistence, like there is no tomorrow. We can do it too, if we are only able to detect what within us is innately screaming to make us each reach the stars: our passion should lead the way! Thomas Edison said, "Our greatest weakness lies in giving up. He most certain way to succeed is always to try just one more time." And it seems successful people also understand this wonderful saying from Sam Levenson: "don't watch the clock; do what it does. It keeps going." Be warned not to fall into the trap of Machiavellian theory, which suggests that cunning, duplicity, and bad faith is acceptable in reaching success, or in other words, that "the ends justify the means." Remember that human decency and righteousness dictate otherwise. As good old Shakespeare teaches in the premise of *Macbeth*, ruthless ambition will lead to its own destruction. No catalyst for wrongdoing should motivate one for a speedy result.

You must be impervious to any enticing ill deed, and at the same time be reminded of what Confucius said: "It does not matter how slowly you go as long as you do not stop." It seems as if those reaching the stars believe in what Friedrich Nietzsche, the German philosopher (1844-1900) had to say: "That which does not kill us makes us stronger."

ESSAY 12

To Be a Wolf or a Sheep?

We ought to be realistic and have enough intelligence to discern the reality of our social and cultural environment. This is an intriguing subject, and as decisive as it is, it should be paid attention to. The "survival of the fittest" mentality has permeated most of our soul and spirit, causing making so many to become less than what humanity deems they should be. Niccole Machiavelli said, "Men rise from one ambition to another: first, they seek to secure themselves against attack, and then they attack others." Having compassion and pity on others is unfortunately not crucial to society's mindset anymore, and regrettably does not materialize.

The motto should be: to act and maneuver like a "sheep," do not be offensive. We need to respect people's rights by being harmless, docile, and non-aggressive. We should not infringe on anyone's sovereignty, and should adapt the culture of helping others in need. On the other hand, make sure to act like a wolf when it comes to defending yourself. Do not let anyone abuse you, or exert any imposition on you or your loved ones.

These days notoriety comes with wealth, power, and influence; most people are conditioned to bypass humanity, becoming wicked in the achievement of their goals, no matter at what cost. There are times we need to behave like sheep, and other times like a wolf. Remember, we live in a cutthroat society, and must be able to protect ourselves. But then, how can we do that if we are weak and not resilient enough to withstand shock—perhaps not intelligent, educated, and wise enough to win?

It is so vital to keep growing, to endure difficulties, to challenge and learn to live with sharks—but we must avoid getting caught and crushed in their jaws. This philosophy can make us stronger and increase our chance of success. We ought to be perseverant, not tenuous or afraid of what life might throw at us. Aim to focus and meditate on hard work and to be the best we can be, but make sure not to lose the grip of what is human. David Hume said, "Where men are the most sure and arrogant they are commonly the most mistaken, giving views to passion without that proper deliberation and suspense which alone can secure them from the grossest absurdities."

We must make sure to act humble and to assist others in need that happen to be in our path, and even help much more when we are glorified and successful. Oscar Wilde puts it this way: "our ambition should be to rule ourselves, the true kingdom for each of us; and true progress is to know more, and be more, and to do more." This trend of thoughts, the zeitgeist of the material world, is unfortunately condescending.

It is quite common to prey on the most vulnerable and the helpless. These thoughts and maladjusted behaviors are prevalent and alive. You should avoid becoming a victim by not getting caught in the crocodiles' mouth. We must understand the warnings and defend ourselves, as there are people among us that camouflage themselves as human beings, when in fact they are beasts; their disguised character tells us otherwise.

This balancing act must be maintained until a serene state of existence is reached, where no atrocities and human pain is either felt or substantiated. As a wise man once said, "there is room for everyone at the rendezvous of victory." Marcus Aurelius stated, "A noble man compares and estimate himself by an idea which is higher than himself; and a mean man, by one lower than himself. The one produces aspiration; the other ambition, which is the way in which a vulgar man aspires."

ESSAY 13

BUDDHA

The word Buddha means "awakened." Buddhism reasons that unless we are enlightened enough to overcome ignorance, we will always have violence since ignorance is accompanied by violence. Because of violence in our mind, we face violence in our world. Being a prince, Buddha experienced extreme luxury and pleasure; he also imposed upon himself extreme austerity, agony, and pain, as he wanted to find an answer to human misery and suffering. His core understanding was that since humans are eventually stricken with old age, sickness, hurt, and death, it is wise to be put through such ordeals, so that perhaps it will make one ready to endure such a bitter life when it is upon us. Buddha lived on one grain of rice daily, stood on one leg, drank his own urine, and tortured himself to the point of death.

He was challenged and put to test with tempting desires as demons tried to break his meditative state of mind and defeat his spirit, but they could not succeed. He became very emaciated and sickly, finally giving up this draconian way of living through suffering. Experiencing the life of plenty at one extreme and bearing so much pain and anguish on the other, finally awakened him. It was only then that he realized that moderation should be the essence—the very key to managing our lives is through love, compassion, and kindness for each other and other creatures. This is the answer to our prayers. Unless these potent human forces are put to practice, only a slight chance remains for man's happiness.

Buddha awakened to a very essential point, this being that "no lopsided load can reach its destiny." Prosperity and success is possible in all we do, if balanced. Buddha, like Einstein, believed that "the most important human endeavor is the striving for morality in our actions." Our inner balance and even our very existence depends on it. Again from Einstein: "only morality in our actions can give beauty and dignity to life." Joseph Conrad, much in line with Buddha's thinking, advises on controlling desires: "A man who has had his way is seldom happy, for generally he finds that the way does not lead very far on this earth of desires which can never be fully satisfied." He believed signs of progress are: "Health, a light body, freedom from craving; these signs indicate progress in meditation." Buddhism believe that quote: "we should not err in this matter of self and other."

Everything is Buddhism (awakening), without exception. Buddhism truly embraces the concept that the extinction of desire will bring an end to suffering. According to Buddha, the way to liberation is by adhering to the eightfold noble path: the right view, right thought, right speech, right action, right livelihood, right effort, right awareness, and the right concentration.

Who's Really at Fault?

When an individual is abused, beaten and neglected as a child, inflicted with pain while growing up, it can affect his/her life significantly. Such people are traumatized, and humiliated, shown no mercy, and have dealt with heinous types of misconduct. When estranged to sympathetic and caring behaviors, it is important to point out that victims would not know there are other sides to humanity that really exist, like love and compassion, kindness and sacrifice and others who are filled with good and positive intentions.

What would you really expect from such a victimized character? Please do not tell me you would expect a miracle such as that person having a good doer's personality with a productive mentality, living a life where everyone and everything will be immune and safe. Please also do not tell me that you do not have the resources or the expertise to and know how to deal with these evils of our time. Such an attitude is conducive to a domino effect—an end result with sinister outcomes as seen and heard over and over again. And this ripple effect escalates and makes life miserable, as shown by the statistics for the crime rate, which keep going up with no hope for recovery. Oh, and furthermore, please do not tell me you are not aware of the real cause to these criminal elements of our society. One thing that I know is that with such treacherous, perilous and broken family backgrounds, victims are exposed to the cruelest of punishments every day. One becomes psychologically damaged from repeated torture and cruelty, and other severely abusive behavior.

That is simply a no-brainer to figure out. Such individuals will most probably act sadistic—numb to the pain and suffering of others—and only there to seek against others by repeating what they went through. They just do not have to have a reason to do what they do. What is constantly hurting them and haunting them like a ghost is their very ominous and painful past. This must be attended to at a grass-roots level, professionally, and not in a clandestine fashion as it is now. These unspeakable troubles of our time, these merciless wrong doers, do not appear out of thin air. You in the position of power and money with leverage and prestige know exactly why society produces these undesirables. And you can do something about it, because you own all the resources necessary to deal with this problem.

Most probably no one chooses to be a criminal unless he or she has been dealt with criminally, by no choosing of his or her own. There is cause for every effect in our lives. When an innocent child is brutally raped and molested, in good conscience, what do you really expect? Civility in mind and manner that is flimsily professed and not backed up with decent intentions or meaningful plans and programs make it a significant challenge. Such a challenge must be fortified with good deeds and sincere, committed actions.

Is your money and wealth so very important to you that they enslave you—making you unwilling to take a decisive and practical approach to deal with this troubling fundamental issue hurting humanity? I wish you would at least attempt to look up the "the categorical imperative" of the maxim from philosopher Kant. As an example, Anthony Kenny, in his book *The Rise of Modern Philosophy,* explicitly states that: "A well-to-do person is asked to help some others who are suffering hardship. He is tempted to respond: What does this matter to me? Let everyone be happy as Heaven wills or as he can make himself. I won't do him any harm, but I won't help him either." But when he considers the *categorical imperative,* he comes to realize that he cannot will "never harm but never help" as a universal maxim because in many situations he will himself need help and sympathy from others.

I do not Know any Better

I want to listen; I do not know how. I want to learn; I do not know how. I want to grow; I do not know how. I want to love; I do not know how. I want to be loved; I do not know how. I want to help, but I do not have the means; I like to blend in and not be isolated, but I do not know how. I want no pride; I do not know how. I want to be happy; I do not know how. I want none of what is belittling me; I do not know how. I do not want to be different; I do not know how. I do not want anyone to point a finger at me; I do not know how.

I do not want to be where I am; I do not know how, I do not want to be labeled based on my having oil, gas, minerals, and other riches; I have nothing to do with it. I do not want to be cast out, but I do not know how. I want to reach and touch someone; I do not know how. I want to pour my heart out; I do not know how. Everywhere I turn, I am struck by peer pressure, and I do not know how to avoid it. I know it is a consumer-oriented society where your products must be sold; but making underhanded efforts to make people become financially exhausted, not giving them a chance to prioritize their lives, is just not decent.

I do not want to be poor and dysfunctional; I do not know how. I want to prove myself positively, but I do not know how. I do not want to be a hero returning from wars; I do not know how. I do not want to be killed in the streets, I do not know how. I do not want to be imprisoned because I do not know any better, and I do not know how. I want a chance to help those who do not know how, but I do not know how.

I do not want to live in the Hood, the ghetto, and to be a gang member; I do not know how. I do not want to be killed in prison, and I do not know how. I wanted to choose where to be born, and whom to be born to; I did not know how. I did not want to be born into poverty and to live with misery, yet I did not know how. Why do you want to challenge me with the "survival of the fittest?" I am already beaten, and I do not know how.

I want to share joy and be part of the human family, but I do not know how; you are too proud to let me in, and I do not know how. I do not want to be a dreamer. It is lonely there, but I do not know how to escape. I want to be real; I do not know how. I do not want to believe in a superior race, nationality, or creed of any type. I want to face discrimination head on, but I do not know how. I do not want to be a victim of your hate because I am different, but I do not know how. I do not want to be brainwashed, yet I just do not know how. I want to be your brother, your sister, and your true friend, but there are too many barriers, and I do not know how. I do not want to be your excuse to go to war with people like me, and I do not know how.

I do not want to return from your wars and be a paraplegic, perhaps mentally disturbed when return from unjust wars. I do not want to need psychiatric help, or commit suicide, but I do not know how. And I do not want to be tortured or executed by some type of Muslim extremist, Sheikh, king, or any other type of government if I do not fight their wars, but I do not know how. I do not believe I should kill innocent people and count them as collateral damages, but I do not know how to stand up against it.

I do not want to listen to those where I live that are supposedly in my corner, but who are serving their own interests and using me and others as guinea pigs, but I do not know how. If you care even a little, it is very simple: we want to be part of your world, and welcome you as part of ours—just let us be who we are meant to be: good human beings and children of the almighty God. I gather God must have believed in you when he determined your destiny to be placed in a position of power and influence, giving you all available means to make a change for the better. And he certainly believed you to be of decent character, not practicing evil to secure your own position of power and excessive wealth and rank. Might this be your test?

We ought to know that there are no excuses any more. The advancement of dynamic technology like the internet, sophisticated media and news, satellites, TV, computer, cell phones, newspapers, magazines, and social media miracles like Google, Yahoo, Twitter, and Facebook has made it very much possible for us all to live in a small world. Very small indeed, for one that knows how and possesses the means to reach and touch everyone in need could make a significant contribution to society.

If you want oil and other natural resources, take them where there are plenty. Do so only if it is for good cause, such as helping other desperate souls, saving lives that are just about to be wasted due to hunger and other basic needs. We should not complain. Such deprived people, including the poor, never had a share of what is known as "commons," or natural resources. Only those in the position of power, influence, and might take what is available, believing that God has blessed them with these reaches. They will and shut anyone up who objects. So you see, *you know how*, and I know I am better off wanting not to be delinquent. I want to be part of your family, and you a part of mine.

Let's all live in one world, one nation under God. Let us prioritize what must be done, which is to interact positively and without bias or discrimination. Our heart feels exhilarated to know you really mean business for the greater good … not for the greatest number, but for all. The last thing you want to do is to label us as having lame excuses, and troubleshooting with laziness. We just need a little push since the odds have been against us from the very beginning, and you were bestowed with all that you wanted—just like having a genie in your corner, exercising supernatural wishes to make your wishes come true.

I just want to do all that I can do to make a difference for a better world. I know I have what it takes, like many others. Just give us a chance to fulfill our wishes. To make it a culture built on the domino effect of love and kindness, with the intent to save humanity and planet Earth—which is already in trouble with all of its inhabitants.

We want to live in peace and harmony. Believe me that there is nothing that should make me, and others like me, any different from you. My heart beats just the same as yours, and yet I wither away with no hope and am prone to pain and suffering. I like to toil and to enjoy the fruits of my labor at the end of the day; and I yearn to be a productive member of society. I also feel embarrassed when I act like an imbecile; and if you are human, you should too. I cast my vote, yet it falls into the abyss, futile. Then a voice from the depths echoes in my head and tell me, "fool, your vote does not count; you have no face.

Becoming Alienated

There is a saying: *KNOWLEDGE MAKES A MAN UNFIT TO BE AN SLAVE.* Ninety-nine percent of our trouble is truly man made. And the only reason for that is ignorance. Unless we are to become enlightened and impressively educated, acquiring wisdom and compassion, we will always be treated as part of the herd. Karl Marx, God bless his soul, explained that we are all alienated 1) from nature, 2) from society, 3) from work, and 4) also we self-alienate. This in turn has affected and caused us all severe ill will with substantial repercussion in our private and public lives. If we are able to choose what is right through wisdom and literacy, I am certain the effects of such alienation would not be significant, or perhaps there would be none, since we are the victims of our own wrongdoing, the environment that live in, and an atmosphere that is coldheartedly planned to keep such a status alive.

To resolve issues that are elusive and affecting humanity in brutal but subtle ways, we need a thorough understanding and an intelligent approach to the root causes of the problems. If so, perhaps then it would be possible to utilize appropriate and constructive measures to remedy our individual and social dilemmas, resolving them by decent and peaceful means.

Being alienated from nature causes a preponderance of human misfortunes, and is certainly displayed dismally in our daily affairs. As humans we can hope for a better future. Not respecting Mother Nature, acting abusive, intrusive, and reckless, polluting the air we breathe, the water we drink, the food we eat, meanwhile overpopulating planet earth is nothing short of barbaric. To exhaust and squander the precious and natural resources that we all depend on (as do future generations), is unbelievably careless and chaotic.

Extreme overproduction and consumption of our natural resources by the powerful and influential industries and multinational corporations has disproportionately affected the poor in ultra-miserable ways. Indigenous inhabitants have been forced out and pushed from their birthplaces and livelihoods. The powerful elites not giving a damn about protecting the precious resources these natives leave behind or about our planet Earth—which by the way is the only one that we have—is far from sensible. Natives leave their farmlands, rain forests, and other organic-producing rural environments and are forced to exodus in unfamiliar and so to speak civilized worlds and metropolitan areas, having no skill, talent, or education to survive this treacherous economy. They become completely disoriented and alienated from the market economy and supposedly from their new lifestyle. They are invisible to the job market, since mainstream jobs require knowledge and complex information that they surely lack; this causes them to become vulnerable to exploitation, becoming enslaved and helpless.

These individuals therefore take on a life of poverty, suffering, and non-productivity, or if they are lucky, minimal paying jobs with no future at all. In most cases they are introduced to the life of crime, human trafficking, and prostitution. All of this ill will happens and victimizes the masses in the name of renovation and economic expansion, which is aimed at maximizing profit and prosperity for the super-rich, no matter at what grave cost. Being practically alienated, and continually so, eventually causes ruin; many examples can be provided, however it is not the intent of this article to further delve into these.

Then alienation from society is to be defiantly addressed since is hazardously affecting our private and public life. So much so that has alienated us all in ways destructive to our true nature as human beings.

Is it our Choice or Are We All Predestined?

Are we already wired to do the things we do? What do you think—do we really have a choice, and are we in control of what is happening? And who is really behind this harmonious, intelligently designed, complexly ordered and self-inclusive universe? A universe that is superbly genius and magnificently justified, that repels the slightest and tiniest chaotic position, and yet is relentlessly and effortlessly managed with marvel and no ultimate wrongdoing?

Let manifest some thought-provoking and probably curious questions. Can we choose when and where, and to whom we should be born? Do we have a choice regarding our birth into a particular demographic? Did we choose whether to enter this life as an animal, a tree of some sort, or and perhaps even another kind of entity?

Has it crossed your mind that everything may be programed and already predestined? Do we have a choice to choose when, how, and where to expire? Do we really have a choice when we die, whether to become recycled, or to otherwise join the infinite spirit of the universe, altered through kinetic energy to become some type of other ontological unit? How is it that we know that mankind, the birds and the bees, pigeons, sparrows, and trees and billions of other species are programed, and are labeled as acting with "instinct?"

Do you not believe that 'acting by instinct" could mean being that we are already instructed to do exactly what we must do? Does this simply mean that we are being programmed, internally encoded to serve a purpose? Do we have a choice not to breathe or stay alive? Can we make a choice not to eat, drink, sleep, and copulate—and millions of other reasonable questions? Look, who are we kidding? We are all planned and predestined. Be it right or wrong, we are victims, also known as the inheritance of the effect on causality.

This whole universe, the cosmos, and billons of other planets and solar systems, the Milky Ways, the stars, and black holes are all orderly, intelligently, and purposefully designed to evolve and to become objectified. Our choices are nothing but illusions; to say we are the masters of our own destiny and in control, is to believe we are not a part of this deterministic universe. It is to insist that we are separate, isolated, and self-contained beings, and not correlated with this whole superbly planned masterpiece. We are not remote islands, as we seem to be. Yes we sometimes do go over, and out of our head and become delusional in believing we can make or break our fate, but that is just bellowing hot air, and it is fictitious.

Every choice we make is already made by our subconscious mind, which is intertwined and undeniably acting in concert with the prevalent and conscious mind of universe. Our deliberately conscious decisions and choices that we supposedly make, are limited; these choices only become solidified consciously as they have already been enacted at the threshold of our subconscious, in our subliminal mind. Are *we* optional in the choices we make? Again the logical question should be—are we a part of this obligatory and systematic plan that is forcefully and deterministically maintained—or not?

The most reasonable answer is obviously not; since we are an undeniable element of this gargantuan strategy, we cannot expect to operate sporadically, unconnected to the source. Intelligent design is premeditated, and operated amazingly artfully, much beyond laser precision. Our universe is so wonderfully disciplined and orchestrated that it cannot fail to astonish all inquisitive and curious minds.

We are not able to and should not contradict this whole natural process if we are to survive, since the programmer is infinitely not visible, is beyond our understanding, and is too far from our human senses to digest. It is of utmost importance to align our conduct and goals as inseparable, and in unison with nature as it is commanded and meant to be. You might ask, if everything is predestined, how does one become strengthened mentally, spiritually, and physically? No one is really able to reach maturity of mind, spirit, and body to become stronger without being contested. We all must endure the bittersweet experiences of life, as it seems that without these experiences, no wisdom or ground breaking knowledge is possible. Our whole existence develops gradually and will perseveringly continue to do so, as this is the way whole systems, such as a universe, must be maintained—in a harmoniously, systematically, and orderly fashion.

It is so tangible and evident that our incessant efforts to try hard are also forced and imposed, since such efforts help and perhaps guarantee our better living and increased productivity for human survival. Without continuous striving and struggles we will be at risk of extinction. It is clear that even these limited choices that we are endowed with need to be an extension of the positive, natural, and love-producing order of the universe. This in turn leaves its mark in a constructive and suitable way on our entire humanity.

Let's reiterate by asking: could our being enlightened and thriving to acquire wisdom, knowledge, and compassion have something to do with freeing ourselves from this deliberate, and mandatory position imposed on us? Of course it seems that way, when we observe other animals, sensing how helpless they are, and realizing that they do not even have the slightest will to choose. Other animals are also entangled in a web of ignorance, devoid of wisdom. And yes, it sure makes a difference when we do our best to grow and become successful, and more than likely progress beyond those who do not. But I do believe that is also predestined by a higher and a supreme planner.

To work hard and to act responsible is not a far cry from destiny being mandatorily implemented. As Karl Marx, the communist philosopher and revolutionary (God bless his soul), once said, "Primates and apes had to constantly jump up working hard to reach trees due to their need for consuming food, like seeds, leaves, cornels, etc. which helped them to straightened their spine." In other words, he believed that work led us to become what we are, ultimately ending up as humans. So you see, even our trying and working hard and doing our best to progress is also undeniably intertwined with how wise and sensible we are, and how open, responsible and inviting we should be to this disciplinary and deliberate force. We must understand this concept, because our futile and irresponsible behavior and actions will be isolated from the forces of the universe, no longer attached to the umbilical cord and the womb of Mother Nature; such action will eventually causes our destruction and demise.

The bottom line is yes; we are all condemned with magnificently justified and constructive determinism. Have in mind the above should not rule out millions of other mysteries or belief systems in our life; it is only fair, and wise, to constantly question why. And if we are already wired to do the things we do, then, why should anyone do anything to improve his or her life?

Yes, that is a reasonable question, and deserves a just answer; of course we all must thrive for a better life, regardless of whether our destiny is calculated or not. And if this mortal life is a test, then we have a better chance of passing rather than not. Then again, predestined or not, we need to understand the importance of the limits in dealing with nature, as compared to our life's endeavors and undertakings, which can bring us to the brink of destruction if not prioritized wisely.

ESSAY 18

Nothingness

We ponder on this controversial issue: are things are created from something, or perhaps made out of nothing? But then, the proper question should more appropriately be addressed as: is nothingness impregnated with an infinite number of things, or not? If not, then a quintillion scientific discoveries that scientists and scholars have divulged and employed should be considered fiction, and no more. It should be acknowledged that our inventions, which we either have already concocted, or hope to excogitate in the future, have stemmed from nothingness and are transmitted into actuality from the unknown. If so, then we should tirelessly dig into nothingness to get closer to the truth, and not let what is explicitly clear become a conundrum of a scientific and philosophical argument.

We perceive and define nothingness according to available human resources and competency. The term "nothingness" can be alarmingly deceptive, since what we know as "nothing" is actually *everything*. Since nothingness is incomprehensible to us at certain times, not discovering and realizing how, when and where, or by whom, nothing is going to give birth to our next scientific breakthroughs. Then we are deluded, based on our limited senses, into believing nothingness as literally meaning immaterial and barren.

The consensus should be in accepting nothingness as the holy grail of creativity—where the real potential lies for things we persist in decoding and eventually conquering. If not, then we are shortsighted in all we have discovered and hope to invent. We are faced with no choice but to delve into the reality of nothing and realize there is no such thing as void. Hence, it would make sense to replace the word nothingness with the word unknown. Since an advanced space digger telescope can reveal a world of magic to the eye, magic that human senses can only dream about, certainly we can see an absence of matter and emptiness without a colossal scientific magnifier. And if the most advanced telescope available to man can only ascertain some of the facts, this only means we must strive for even better technology, to more effectively measure the facts and make human dreams reality.

To say life came from nothing is honestly an insult to reason. This literally means that God is in charge of the womb of what we know and grant as emptiness— which in contrary, is filled with propitious prospects. That God gave birth to all there is and all there will ever be. Through the eyes of quantum physics, which represents the unseen world, renowned physicists like Niels- Bohr and many of his colleagues accepted that "atomic uncertainty is truly intrinsic to nature: the rules of clockwork might apply to familiar objects such as snooker balls, but when it comes to atoms and quarks, string theory, and other subatomic particles, the rules are those of roulette." Many scientists believe these subatomic particles are being thrown around by an unseen ocean of microscopic forces.

It is therefore apparent that we must adhere to the bounds of our senses to become acquainted with and to comply with the world outside of us. Although as humans we cannot reconnaissance with what is beyond our ability and knowledge to decipher this should not mean that there is no magic in the air, or that we need to quit searching for miracles. Since history of evolution should validate human mind that progresses into dynamic stages of enlightenment where boundaries are graciously torn and miracle-like discoveries become norms. It seems beautiful minds are impacted with premonition, and are mandated with a mission somewhat gynecological in nature—figuratively peering into the womb of mother nature, encouraging her to give birth to yet another treasure. Such treasures unveil the mysteries of nature's obscurities and emancipate man from the clutches of ignorance.

Our curiosity into the realms of speculation and probability is fostered and potentially backed up by hidden agendas, subsequently conveyed into the unknown—ready to be exploited and to ultimately burst into reality. This transference is, of course, inclined to action through passion, human drive, and time consumed, and is keen enough to detect the maturity of the idea to determine the magnificent moment of delivery. This is further encouraged by hope, perseverance, and bearing hardship through many trials and errors; and then occasionally hits the bulls-eye, providing stepping stones for other miracle-like disclosures. And sometimes a huge leap into successful challenges where our struggle in bettering human life pays off generously.

About Love

We are not commodities; we are human beings with souls, designed so delicately to have emotion that can pierce into the very core of our existence. We are an undeniable part of cosmic spirit; love and kindness aligns with our positive energy and consciousness. When one is under the spell of emotion, hypnotized by feelings, no amount of logic and savviness of mind or intellect, can ever halt one from doing the unthinkable. Call it creation, evolution, or call it as you please.

It is an undeniable fact that the God inside is by nature made to love and to belong. When human beings are depleted of love and caring, we rebel and exercise our lower self, hence acting ugly and depraved. This manifests itself in many shapes and forms, some of which can put the most vicious animals to shame. We are made to love, and with a need to belong. Without these we rebel and defy what humanity stands for in the name of reason and even law. Love is an innate force, and so potent that it can either make or break us—but it is not clearly understood. Since many are fed with the hallucinogenic drugs of conditioning and do not see the underlying cause of man's misery, sometimes they only recognize the effects. This means that I cannot shy away from the truth, since I feel like a dead man walking without good souls to connect with, and a sense of belonging. I believe that is why some hardened psychologists recommend isolation and solitary confinement to punish prisoners, which I am afraid leaves a devastating effect on them rather than making a difference for the better, and does not play a constructive role in their therapeutic regiments.

Love is the utmost important part of our human experience; it is the most imperative time in our lives. Love comes in different tastes and flavors, but is always colorful and exciting. As Deepak Chopra states, "our biological response begins to self-regulate when we are in love; it is an expression of the soul, which is timeless. It comes in different shapes and forms. It can happen with a significant other, with parents and siblings, with love for art, music, paintings, beautiful scenery, etc." And as Tegur said (Rabindranath 1861-1941 Indian poet), "love is not a mere sentiment, is the ultimate truth at the heart of creation."

The only time we are not concerned about death—that at least it does not cross our subconscious mind—is when we are truly in love. It is when we are lost in the moment, where hours become seconds, and the seconds are not noticed. If you disagree, then you have not experienced life the way it meant to be. How potent and sacrosanct this heavenly word called love it is! And in reality only when we are given a chance to exist, can we positively propel forward, authenticating our nature. Since love should be an undeniable facet in our lives, when it is fabricated and abused it then all the good things we stand for as human beings go topsy-turvy. Unless each and every one of us reaches love's full potential, there will be absolutely be no hope to reach serenity of mind and meaningful coexistence. Have you not noticed how time flies when you are in love, how carefree your spirit becomes? It is as if you never want to leave what you are delightfully experiencing. This complacency is prevalent in modern cultures and societies, as we notice the diminishing of love in its true essence. It is very much mind-boggling.

The most disturbed soul could be healed and revitalized if only given a chance to love and to be loved. Yes, we also can be brought down by our demons, but only in the absence of love, which is an entity we humans all have the potential to possess—and abundantly so. Structural violence is the root cause of our behavioral violence, and is designed to keep us from the God-given jewel of feeling love for one another.

But even love must surely have an unbiased environment, where it can be activated to grow. If the opportunity and the atmosphere to bloom is not furnished, it will be suffocated from its inception and perhaps never be felt. When hate is the only alternative manufactured, and is deliberately set to serve a purpose for the few in charge, we call it divide and conquer. Shakespeare put it this way, "love all, trust a few, do wrong to none." How then are such characters motivated, no matter what the reason, to cause these bitter conditions—and not really be disturbed by the resulting violence in behavior? Is it love, or lust and an urge for sexual fulfillment that should be prioritized? The word love has a sacrosanct meaning; it is interactively bonded with the spiritual and heavenly phase of nature and humanity. Love cannot be fully manifested and truly expressed in a materially-based society.

It becomes very difficult to distinguish between love and lust, as there are many fine lines between them that are hard to discern. Yes, it is a fact that being loved and loving someone in return is very potent, and perhaps one can lose his or her mind over it if not accomplished. Potent also are sexual urges, infatuation, lust, attachments, sympathy, attraction, affection, and many other human feelings that could very easily be mistaken with being in love. Aristotle said, "Love is composed of a single soul inhabiting two bodies." In modern societies, people are constantly bombarded with self-preservation, with a "me first" attitude, which very much propagates a culture of individualism.

It is very hard to make sense of the meanings of tolerance, compromise, self-sacrifice, devotion, patience, and other components that are truly identified with sincere love. It is of paramount importance to recognize that love gradually builds, just like the unconditional love of a mother for her baby that is pampered from infancy, and the platonic love of a brother, sister, mother, or father. The expression "love at first sight," does not serve its meaning; no love can be conveyed at first sight, although perhaps liking and sex can. The desire for sexual intimacy is also a very powerful human feeling. Sigmund Freud (1910), the father of psychology, has empathically said that it is the corner stone of human interest. And could very well be a fad, and so to say an exaggerated zeal, and not love at all.

Most philosophers, anthropologists, neurosurgeons, psychologists, sociologists, and religious people unanimously believe and define love as a cognitive event that is said to have three main ingredients: intimacy, commitment, and passion. This definition has forgotten the fourth and main ingredient: the time it takes for such a marvelous event to reach maturity. Be careful not be mistakenly conflate sex with love in an environment that confuses the mind.

"A lover knows only humility, he has no choice.
He steals into your alley at night, he has no choice.
He longs to kiss every lock of your hair, don't fret,
he has no choice. In his frenzied love for you, he longs
to break the chains of his imprisonment,
he has no choice." **RUMI**

We are an undeniable part of the universe and our natural life. Phenomena in both our universe and nature happen gradually. Science can testify that time plays a very crucial factor in making things happen, and in a fundamentally disciplined way. It would be most advantageous to model the fascinating ways of nature as our teacher. When something as moral, spiritual, holy, and wonderful as love is to happen, it certainly requires time to mature. If you do not believe me, simply look at the statistics of partners that utter: "I taught him," or "she loved me;" that is when the fine line between love and sex is not identified. So many divorces and crimes happen, painstakingly so in love-related events. One only has to listen to the everyday news, which is filled with victims of love-related issues and sagas. How easily people give up their soul for the love of money, when targeting their prey in the name of love, objectifying their inhumane goals. Eric Eromm says, "Immature love says: I love you because I need you. Mature love says I need you because I love you."

You are what you believe; the veracity and the correctness of what you believe depends on how enlightened you are. You become enlightened to behold the truth, and the truth will set you free. To know that true love manifests itself is when we overcome our pride and other troubling cultural harms that play active roles in forcing us into something we are not. WOur feelings and emotions cry out loud to escape from behind the iron bars of society-imposed cages—cages of selfishness and prejudice in which they build up pressure, threatening to explode. We want to reveal the frustration and abandonment that confuses and entangles us in a web of uncertainty, but then this is hard to do without the professional assistance of expert psychologists who help us to work through love-related issues and other emotional disturbances and disorders. If we are ever able to show what we are actually made of and manifest it in a true sense, we will most definitely have a plausible clue of where God actually resides. According to H. Jackson Brown, Jr., "Love is when the other person's happiness is more important than your own." Per Plato the Greek philosopher, "At the touch of love, everyone becomes a poet."

What Are We?

Our daily engagements in having a functional life are as demanding as they are time consuming; because of this, most people are numb toward exploring "what we are," or perhaps do not even care about to reference it as important at all. This is strikingly sad. Unless we can correctly assess the answer to what we are, the subtle captivity inherent in the lack of such knowledge will negatively affect our individual and social interactions and welfare. Regardless of how advanced we seem to be in our modern lifestyle, the negative repercussions will eventually impact us all.

Historically there are two major viewpoints on this rather intricate question. One is the materialistic view, which holds that humans are physical, behaviorist beings that act mechanically in response to external stimuli, experiencing a robotic-like reaction to environmental processes. This view leaves no room for closeness to God, spiritual training, or any soul-searching activities. Science is materially based, and looks at the world objectively; it and cannot explain it subjectively and cannot understand the way innate forces operate. Materialists are trying to locate the center of awareness, not realizing that cosmic awareness is predominant and is magically experienced through many forms and shapes: animals, plants, humans, planets, stars and galaxies, through the billions of universes and so on. What really matters is how we express it, Humans express consciousness dynamically, and are at the pinnacle of this awakened chain. The unexplained epiphany happens when the essence of the phenomenal world is not matter, but consciousness. When our thoughts and awakening mind elevates a few degrees, it is then that what we knew as a miracle becomes reality. Cosmic energy makes our cognition and experiences possible.

On the other extreme we have idealists, who accept and proclaim the physical world does not exist; everything is just perception, and the material world is nothing more than our imagination. Which answer we grasp over the other, either materialist or idealist, affects the way we think and how we respond to sometimes very delicate matters that we might face in our lives. From a mechanical and reductionist perspective, man is perceived as a reduced entity; we are being lowered in status to resemble hardware and machinery, thus are better qualified in our robotic programming to deal with environmental changes.

That, I say, is rather a senseless indoctrination, short-sighted in definition of man's attributes and a deadened evaluation of human beings' characters. Let's give the materialist view the benefit of the doubt. If so, should we remove the idea of having a programmer or not? If not, are we all programed the same and therefore must react uniformly to external stimuli? And if yes, what are the differences, if any, that distinguish us from lower species of animals that behave homogeneously by instinct? Which then means that any other human attributes and characteristics should not be immune to external changes or counted as intrinsically worthy, other than being solely behavioristic and instinctual.

Either way, there must be an innately animated force that is conscious and sensitive to outside changes, causing us to respond accordingly. There is also the need for some proprietor of awakening power in the animal kingdom to spur millions of them into "survival of the fittest behaviorism," propelling beasts with brute strength to retaliate for being hunted by humans, who savagely kil their victims by overpowering them, assisted by camouflaging and stealthy maneuverability. Which by the way would become a recipe for disaster to follow, if we were to become a disciple of atheistic views, and hence regarded as "mechanically" oriented entities.

You might contest that the survival of the fittest mentality and belief is accepted as truth by many Godly societies as we speak. To speak to that, I can reassure you we are dealing with hypocrisy in action by many, where self-centeredness and greed has taken over; the effects of this are worse than the work of any honest atheist or materialistic individual. The question which remains is: do human beings have intrinsic values? Do animals have intrinsic values and experience feelings and emotion deeply as humans do? When plants react to external stimuli like rain, sunshine, fertilizers, proper gardening, when they bear fruits with nutritional value, and eventually dry out and die, are they also behaviorist, since they react to environmental changes too? The point is, many existent beings react to outward catalysts, including humans, but it sure does not mean we are intrinsically barren, as we are far from it.

When you evaluate people from a mechanical point of view and deplete them of feelings and emotions, do they have the right, for example, to seek justice and react by taking revenge if one's innocent family is slaughtered by criminals? And if yes, then what exactly is it that pushes one to want revenge? Finally, do animals feel and react the same way towards such injustice when their kind is beheaded for dinner?

When one covers a ticking bomb and explodes to pieces, saving others from getting killed, is it the outside stimuli forcing one to sacrifice his or her life to such extent, or is it because of intrinsic values? If it is because of external stimuli, why would everyone present not be inclined to perform such extreme self-sacrifice? Or when one pulls his fingers so fast from a burning hot stove, reacting quickly to an outward incidence, so that one does not get burned, as compared to when someone jumps to his or her death trying to save a child's from getting killed by an oncoming bus? Should these two reactions to external stimuli be considered the same, and if not, what causes the extent of such sacrifice inherent to the latter one?

Do all people react the same to: fear of punishment, rewards, death, worries, justice, revenge, self-sacrifice, excitement, love, beauty, ambition and risk-taking, courage, hunger, wealth, poverty, loyalty, caring, kindness and compassion, philanthropy, benevolence, in giving and generosity, intuition, IQ and intelligence, insightfulness, greed, uprising, or when they are discriminated against? Are the reactions exclusive to each person and situation, or common to all of us? If not common, why not? I thought we as members of the human species should react the same to particular occurrences, since we are all mechanically labeled, and descended to behave instinctually. How about when a soldier volunteers to be sent to the front line at a time of war—is it the same motivation as someone who spies for the enemy, no matter how many innocent lives are endangered or are wasted?

Do our emotions and feelings, our thoughts and dreams, our laughter and joy, our happiness, our pain and anguish, the language in which we communicate, and the sacrifices we make have weight, affect chemical composition, or occupy space? If yes, I thought only what carries weight, has chemical composition and occupies space is manifested and bound to as materialistically real—as compared to agendas which are not manifested the same, and are considered as superficially idealistic. Look, there are intrinsic human values that are explored and put to work by heavenly characters every day and many times over that stem from human compassion and caring, from love and devotion, from loyalty and sacrifice, from dignity and honesty, from passion and longing for justice. If some hard-headed ideologue behaviorist wants to turn a blind eye to blunderings and prove a mirage-like situation real, then well-known wisdom should apply: if it looks like a duck, swims like a duck, and quacks like a duck, then it is probably a duck. And if we are behaviorists who should mechanically react to environmental changes and automatically respond the same to circumstances facing us, why would anyone need to think or seek solutions to one's problems? We shouldn't have to, since we are supposedly programed to act by instinct, collectively interacting in a herd-like manner to address any auspicious or dire circumstances.

We ought to cling to the core of humanity, which contains the remnants of stardust as recently claimed by cosmic scholars, physicists and space scientists. Since humanity should identify with people's pain and suffering, with their hunger and displacement from their abode and habitat, from natural tragedies that might have faced them, it should not let them die in vain. It takes time to discard "junk knowledge" and ill-received information deliberately instilled in people's heads for the benefit of the few that sadly have become blinded with the love of money, and numb to human compassion. Their incriminating behavior forces the survival of fittest mentality on desperate masses of people, making it a cutthroat society rather than creating a culture of cooperation. A true culture of compassion has proven to be immensely positive and very productive in bringing people closer together; this would certainly make a huge difference in improving people's lives, their prosperity, and in honoring God.

Let us capitalize on what in heaven's name we are all about. We are about light, we are about love, we are about healing. Stop brewing evil in the name of mankind, misleading them to believe they are cursed, and perhaps do not deserve to live. Because you have appropriated and accumulated so much wealth, then you have been blessed and ought to have a clear conscious—this is far from the truth. Your misconduct is exactly why atheists and behaviorists, agnostics, and the like are emboldened to doubt God. Because of the consequences of your misdeeds, mankind is ignorant enough to hold God responsible for human misery and their own pain and suffering. When Jesus was asked by his disciples, "Where do we come from?" he said, "We come from light." Contemporary scientists, with all of their might, scientific research, and magnificent telescopes are now attesting to what Jesus said more than two thousand years ago.

When Lack of Sex and Money Hurts You

Looking at love and sex traditionally, it should remind us of family oriented societies that are embodied with love and sexual relation that are expected to happen after marriage is consummated. Ideally, in such a society, monogamy would be encouraged because it becomes a vanguard in intimacy and marital relationships. Wrong or right it is not my place to judge, but from my personal perspective, the whole concept of monogamous marriage is questionable at this contemporary age. Since our sexual feelings and emotions are innate needs, researchers have shown that in some cases yesterday's standards for closeness can leave unhealthy side effects if not adequately fulfilled and appropriately dealt with.

These side effects then morph into abnormalities that can disturb one's equanimity, possibly requiring professional medical and psychological attention, as their repercussions can be very harmful to society and oneself if not detected at earlier stages of development. These feelings are normal and we should cherish them as vital parts of who we are that ought to be understood and respected. They should not be taken as taboos, depicted as sinful, or subjects that we are reticent to talk about. Historically, marriage and family are perhaps in accord with cultural standards, where sex is designed to happen after the marriage, but in my view, monogamy is a questionable principle, especially in today's world.

This premise leaves one to wonder if sexual feelings should be culturally orchestrated and followed as they were handed down by our predecessors, or if they are to be revalued in dynamic ways and altered to modern human standards. One positive result would be that so much infidelity, cheating, hypocrisy, lying, and family related crime and jealousy would not happen. Our emotions and intimacies are coherent with human nature, which naturally stem from within. Following routes designed to manipulate our thoughts and feelings, however, sometimes causes those feelings to be abandoned, while we live contrary to the essence of our nature, thus unwisely choking our natural desires, which can result in unresolved psychological complexities. It is our human nature to pursue liberty and happiness, and we have the right to choose whatever endeavors in which we wish to engage, which should not exclude love and sex. My belief is that our emotional needs are to be positively inspired within the affinity of freedom of integration.

Multiple partners and polygamy are perhaps not practical and immoral and may be even considered sordid. The other extreme, however, is to end up trapped with a life-time partner, or significant other, where one's thoughts, emotions, love, happiness, respect, trust, and devotion are no longer intact and have been depleted of joy. Why then should any modern society propagate and foment such an outdated idea as marriage? Could it be our pride and sticking to what is customary even if is not making sense any more, and not compatible with today's time parameters? If not, then, what is the cause to having so much family violence and rampant marriage-oriented trouble, causing so much frustration with no viable solution available? We are urgently in need of finding a resolute alternative to the madness of the epidemic of divorce, resulting in millions if not billions of single parenthood dilemmas.

Arguably, one could predict the eradication of the single-family unit, or household-oriented society, which could disappear like dinosaurs. When digging into many of our problems, we should notice what we are faced with is the outcomes of perhaps thousands of years of long-time traditions. These were manipulated and designed by our predecessors from antiquity and have gradually been handed down, even to modern times. This reality occurs, despite the fact of having so many matrimonial related problems and family violence, much of which arguably stems from the culture of thinking in terms of traditional relationships. Many western societies have not experienced traditional cultures, so detrimental to people's life; that effects marriage for worst and since, religion has a lot to do with it, as it plays a huge role at the very core of people's lives.

Horrifying issues like honor killings of sometimes innocent young wives and daughters, arranged marriages, forcing minors to consummate marriage, male permitted to have four to five or more wives with religious backings. And how many young girls and women either commit suicide each year, and or run away because they are forced into unwanted marriage, but are sold in the name of marriage? I am also certain that people are aware of family violence skyrocketing, and so on. Do you know girls as young as five years old, as they still are playing with dolls, are arranged into marriage to forty, fifty, sixty years old men, in which some of these very under age females die at the horrors of their first night of consummation of their so called marriage. To see these atrocities first hand, in many corner of the world and hundreds more troubling situation imposed on helpless girls and women, will sure create much more sympathy to these human sufferings. Human right organizations are still trying to put a stop to murdering brides by burning. According to front line magazine, India. Quote: Bride-burning accounts for the death of at least one woman every hour in India. "We also call it dowry death," says Donna Fernandes, the founder of Vimochana, a women's rights organization established in Bangalore in 1975 with the aim of preventing violent against women, she says quote:

"In many cases the husband's family decide after the marriage has taken place that the original dowry was not sufficient. They know the bride's family is vulnerable, because of subjugated role of women in our society, and what begins is a process of extortion. Demands for money turn into threats of violence, and when the family can't pay any more, the bride is killed."

This burning brides practices also occurs when the husband to new bride dies for one reason or another. Did you know female genital mutilation known as "clitoridectomy" is still quite common in many parts of the world, especially in African nations? Where they perform in removing the entire clitoris, or part of it. This demonic practices are done while many young girls ready to be brides are forcefully held down, despite their rigorous and gut-wrenching effort to get away, while someone with a razor sharp knife executes this malicious and inhuman task.

On one hand, people's choice in cutting loose is sometimes hijacked by wild notions such as unfettered hedonism, the results of which present monumentally difficult challenges. On the other side of spectrum, however, there are many who never get to experience marriage and nuptials, which in some religiously zealous societies is the only way to love someone and to have sex. In these situations, females are the true victims of this kind of nonsense and way of life, leaving many of them no choice but to live a celibate and "nun like" existence through sexual inactivity and abstinence forced upon them. The proponents of some of the strictest matrimonial cultures make it appear as if God himself prescribed such devilish medicine, since millions upon millions of females are essentially cursed and pay a heavy price for such wrongful-minded zealotry. Too many of them are destined to never taste the most sacred of human feelings of love and parenthood, which are deemed to stem only from marriage. Where could anyone find social civility in that, I wonder? We ought to bear in mind not everyone is famous or has enough notoriety, wealth, or power to easily resolve their sexual dilemmas.

The world witness's daily, that famous celebrities and other prominent and powerful figures engage in many marriages in their life time, and with unlimited freedom to vacillate among many choices available to them, and to casually choose and to dispose them so called significant others late in a whim and as they fancy. The irony is that these high rollers in many societies, movie stars and the like, are setting examples that one day could become substantiated and accepted as the new cultural norm. Many new ideas and changes have occurred perhaps gradually at inception, but eventually were accelerated to arrive at their objectives. Bear with me as I like to momentarily detour and talk about Marx views on cultural issues, which he constituted as "the super structure" or the cosmetic part of any structured and class differentiated society which the infrastructural base and the mode of production are the real cause to super structure, from different era in human history.

What Marx principally believed should happen was fundamental economic changes, and if so, then, other social changes which he called superstructure will automatically be pursued. Marx defined SUPERSTRUCTURE as quote: the ideologies that dominate a particular era, all that "men say, imagine, conceive," including such things as "politics, laws, morality, religion, metaphysics, etc." (Marx and Engels, German Ideology.) For Marx, the superstructure is generally dependent on the modes of production that dominate in a given period.

If this was to occur, then, the productive forces become impregnated with new ideas in guiding the masses of their rights which will substantiate the inevitable struggle and clash of titans—between economically differentiated classes of haves and have not's—which in turn would bring about a revolution and a new world free of exploitation.

Marx characterized civilized societies as the economic base and political societies as the political superstructure. Marx claimed the intrinsic of the base–superstructure concept as quoted and defined: "In the social production of their existence, men inevitably enter into definite relations, which are independent of their will, namely [the] relations of production appropriate to a given stage in the development of their material forces of production. The totality of these relations of production constitutes the economic structure of society, the real foundation, on which arises a legal and political superstructure, and to which correspond definite forms of social consciousness. The mode of production of material life conditions the general process of social, political, and intellectual life. Marx, he said quote: "It is not the consciousness of men that determines their existence, but their social existence that determines their consciousness." At a certain stage of development, the material productive forces of society come into conflict with the existing relations of production or — this merely expresses the same thing in legal terms — with the property relations within the framework of which they have operated hitherto(up to this or that time.) From forms of development of the productive forces, these relations turn into their fetters, which then begins an era of social revolution.

The changes in the economic foundation lead, sooner or later, to the transformation of the whole, and immense superstructure. In studying such transformations, it is always necessary to distinguish between the material transformation of the economic conditions of production, which can be determined with the precision of natural science, and the legal, political, religious, artistic, or philosophic — in short, ideological forms in which men become conscious of this conflict and fight it out. Just as one does not judge an individual by what he thinks about himself, so one cannot judge such a period of transformation by its consciousness, but, on the contrary, this consciousness must be explained from the contradictions of material life, from the conflict existing between the social forces of production and the relations of production."

Marx's base, determines superstructure axiom, however, requires qualification:

- The base is the whole of productive relationships, not only a given economic element, e.g. the working class. Historically, the superstructure varies and develops unevenly in society's different activities; for example, art, politics, economics, etc.
- The base–superstructure relationship is reciprocal; Engels explains that the base determines the superstructure only in the last instance.

This should remind one of the cliché which says: "if it sounds too good to be true, then perhaps isn't." The bottom line to utopian of Marxism, takes a miracle to make it possible, a miracle of knowledge and understanding, a miracle of education and compassion, a miracle of wisdom and sacrifice, a miracle of truly changing heart with kindness, with embracing insightfulness, and willingness to help. You see, what Marx believed in, it boils down to, quote: "From each according to his ability, to each according to his need." This cannot come true, while the average intelligent is still raw, and such extent of self-sacrificed still a utopia and very rare, especially since the individualism philosophy is the overall cultural norm which is still very much craved and praised. But then, Marx was not a fool, he was a genius in his own right, and he knew it was extremely difficult to bring about a cultural revolution which would make the expression of each according to his ability which should contribute to society, and must take only according to one's need, not yet a reality, but they immaturely were counting on the "dictatorial of proletariat." I am sure Marx, Lenin and others did not mean the present Soviet Union, Cuba or China, when they talked about actual communism, and how they treat masses of people, not to exclude people's marital affairs, which is a farcical. Because many victims of human trafficking and sex slaves are the products of the so called socialism countries.

One might think to identify with such discipline, and thought provoking idea as "Marxism," should perhaps free us form hazards of cultural taboos and to grant humanity immunity from the clutches of stupefied customs; which are yet dysfunctional and ill maneuvered, but still play a significant role in many societies as we speak, which are known to be part of the super structural domain.

This cannot practically be perceived where there are many other questionable and active variables in human nature that we are involved with and meshed in. And since for any dynamic and revolutionary change to occur, we must have the ingredient, and the expertise available to us to make it happen. An Stable social revolution either economic or any other dynamic social, economic and culture changes, not to exclude monogamy in marriage, or any other gender and sexual related issues needs to stem out from top-down and not from down-top manner. I believe the changes need to incept and come from top- down, rather than with bottom up trend. Because those who are to be responsible for such vital and dynamic task, must have the knowledge and information; they should pertain proper education, with financial leverage and economical skills, they need to have the wit and the wisdom along with having mental and psychological competencies, and the courage to instigate modern and constructive social, economic and cultural changes.

Not through any dictatorial rules, and by force, which should not exclude "dictatorial of proletariat" since it seems the shortcomings and deficiencies in their knowledge, and education, the lack of skills in management and communication creates a big vacuum, which I am afraid is mended through coercion and appropriation and annexing ownership, hence making "dictatorship of proletariat" literally, a cultural and legal social norm. Certainly a wrong patch to uphold a revolution, rather than by enlightenment, inference, and by peaceful means and dialogue which are the essence and the attributes of a civilized world. Perhaps a renaissance and revolution in new ideas are to fundamentally mature and contextually be accepted before any change could dynamically materialize. Especially on sensitive subject as marriage and sex related issues which are still filled with taboo like beliefs and behaviors, even at this twenty first century.

But, then again any ratiocination (the process of reasoning), and thought invoking concepts are bound to education and constructive training, which are ignored and misrepresented. Where skill enrichment, and wisdom with good dialogues, patient, perseverance, peaceful and professional interactions, money well allocated and well spent, are the keys to success, and since quality attributes as such should be the main component to resolve intricate social and economic agendas, or any other conundrum oriented subject. Unfortunately the idea of maximizing profit, and "the idea of time is money" outweighs the welfare of society which are staccato (disconnected, cut short), they are put at the backburner, and are not paid attention to, for saving life and families.

Love and sex are biologically and emotionally oriented needs which must not be ignored. And when deprived from intimacy and sexual intercourse, meshed in with poverty, then it can blind one from the serenity in thought and manner. Which in turn can devoid one from etiquette behavior and civilized action. People should not be constricted with rules that are not practically sound, and not docile with today's modern life style, which are the cause of so many social ill since they practically malfunction. Old and out dated cultures of thought and norm, depravity in Wisdom, devoid of literacy and education, deprived of a sound mental and psychological behavior, lack of morality and righteousness, financially distressed, and being raised in a poverty stricken neighborhood, barren in spirituality and compassion, feeling of guilt and bereft of loved and sexual communion not conducive to satisfying coitus, an abusive environment, jealousy and peer pressure, not having access to a decent role model and socially skilled personal, insecurity

And feeling of not being accepted or belonged, pride, incompetency to adequately manage the off shoot of such ill character referenced. Can be triggered to cause trouble and malice where one can easily be prone to act like an animal and to employ one's lower self, inflicting harm to self and the society.

Problems occur when we are deprived of having a warm and caring atmosphere to fulfill our sexual and emotional needs that can negatively affect us for worse. Since the culture of thinking must accord with innate way we feel, and relax enough to accommodate an environment to constructively encourage tasteful sexual behavior, where people wouldn't masquerade their true feelings and for not becoming a commodity in demand of sexual market.

In a congested atmosphere where it is a taboo to freely express one's feelings, which sexual emotion are unwisely restrained can eventually lead to debauchery and sexual misconduct, and sex slave with senseless erotic behaviors that is not healthy. In which we should witness signs of abnormal sexual and malevolent actions where the indicators can manifest themselves conspicuously at the very young age. Surging hormones and lack of knowledge in human sexuality and relationship, not attuned and matured in ethical perspectives and not acting higher self, and perhaps impacted by peer pressure, Can embroil and throw one into disorderly conduct. Which should not be considered an impropriety, or disgraceful and to be laughed at, rather it needs to be sensibly pursued with giving skillful therapy and encouraged with a positively receptive attitude in caring environment.

Irrationally inhibiting people's feelings, can significantly suppress and curtail our natural tendencies which could result in reclusiveness, despondency and other malice and ill effect. What Freud believed was to dig into the distorted and frustrated patient's past since the trouble is the reminiscence of neglected, untreated, and suppressed sex related issues which has brought about pathological and the hysteria in the patient needing treatment. Many of social, cultural, political, norms are engulfed with chores and expectation of before and after marriage that are not fashionable and in conflict with interests of modern society and its expectation.

Our mental and psychology, hormonal and physiology, our love and intimacy, our sexual relations, sing a different song, which gradually forces the tradition barriers to break, and the advanced societies are the pioneer of this social sexual revolution. And rightly so, since we are to some extent the product of our environment, which has effected our relations through social institution of marriage and family life, as it is structured in ways, that some of its participants perhaps are not lucky enough to find partners for life through wedding and private relationship.

It is progressive not to see these social sexual interactivities as derogatory (insulting and demeaning), if not privately manifested. Since in many instances sexual activities (prostitution) occur when situation turn ugly on people impacting them with lives most troublesome and abysmal (hideous) incidents and very difficult to bear issues. And not always a product of a choice that can be sudden in victimizing anyone. Perhaps one day we will reach where these human connections and social sexual behaviors will be considered only as an "state of mind," where so much hypocrisy and contradiction would not happen making it a theater type life style, where authenticity of character is lost, and replaced with quack and dishonesty just to survive and perhaps to belong. And where people would be culturally and financially comfortable enough in not becoming commodities of huge profit base sex industries, since it is inclined to leave its foot print in demise in people's life, and with horrific outcomes.

There are many professional diagnosis that relate to individuals with dire mental and psychological diseases when they become deprived of a loving and emotionally attentive environment. If so, a preemptive strike at the heart of such anticipated problems is necessary at the very young age. So that the history of a person would be written in a more healthy promising ways and with optimism.

We need not to unleash and let the problem strayed which later on can threaten our societies with sexual psychopath and psychopathic behavior. Individuals with neuroses, hysteria, psychotic, and with many other complexity and mental disorder acting pervert and in rage, and causing rape, incest, child abuse, pedophiles, prostitution, fondling and molestation, and host of other psycho sexual disorder (serial killers), also incurring horrifying and sometimes incurable sexual diseases.

Disorderly sexual behaviors and misconducts are relatively mitigated in the "upper echelon" of the society especially in many developing nations, since they have the accessibility to sexual freedom, knowledge and literacy, able to afford professional medical help, proper guidance and education, as they are leveraged with wealth and financial might to correct bad consequences, which entitles them to higher rate of success and probabilities to survive perhaps radical sexual encounters.

Let's look at some alternatives that supposedly are to cure mental malaise and difficulties. "Skinnerian psychology" believes in a view of behavior modification that says quote: man is simply an animal and we must treat him as such. Skinner believed man to be nothing more than an animal and thus fails to see man as a being who was created in the image of God (Gen. 1:27). Also at the other extreme we can witness: "Rogerian psychology" is based on humanistic thought, namely, that the solution to man's problems lies within the man himself. "Christians" reject this viewpoint on the basis of its humanistic presuppositions alone -- it begins with man and ends with man and asks us to accept the aberrant (abnormal) behavior of people without any sort of judgment.

However, the Scriptures specifically command that quotes: we "judge with righteous judgment" (John 7:24). The main goal of Rogerian psychology is to make people feel good about themselves, regardless of their sins. However Mr. David Padfield says quote: There can be no question that guilt is one of the great destroyers of the soul. Guilt, whether imagined or real, leads individuals on a downward spiral which will destroy their relationships in life and render them worthless in the kingdom of God.

An individual with a guilty conscience often becomes bitter and lashes out to those who are trying to help. Sin is at the root of the problem, for sin leads to guilt and depression, and sinful handling of sin further complicates matters leading to greater guilt and deeper depression. Proverbs 5:22 well describes this progression of sin, "His own iniquities entrap the wicked man, and he is caught in the cords of his sin." However, guilt can be a good thing when it brings one to a realization of one's sins. This types of talk should be expected from a so called divine doctrine which sadly believes quote: "we are born with sin and not a clean slate."

Further, he carries on the removal of Guilt, Quote: Either you can have your sins forgiven by the blood of Christ, or you can allow the guilt of your sins to destroy you. Suppose you were driving in a car and the water temperature gauge on the dashboard turned red and said your car was overheating? You could stop the car, go to the trunk and get a hammer, and then smash the gauge to pieces -- and then go on your way. However, you will not get far -- destroying the red warning light will not remove the problem -- it simply masks it for a little while.

Your conscience is a lot like the red warning light on the dashboard -- it tells you when you have a problem that needs attention. You can go to a Freudian psychologist and have your conscience smashed, seared and destroyed -- but your problem remains. Your problem is sin and it will never get better on its own! It is possible for one to sear their conscience (1 Tim. 4:2). Any competent psychologist, psychiatrist in related field can attest to the above doctrine and their respond to sex and human feelings as not "emotionally intelligent," and not worthy of any medical and scientific credibility. From the above doctrine and their analogy on how to accord with intricate mental health related problems, and how they should be treated.

I can only gather one thing which is: not to be surprised at the mess we are in where sex, and violence are rampant since we have not adequately faced them and significant solution are yet to be materialized. The proponent of such unfounded beliefs cannot fathom we have reached the age of consciousness where superstitious should backfire since alike doctrines are only mocked. Hence, we ought to be thankful to the "separation of church and state" and for the freedom of thought and speech that ensures scientific lectures and theories to become comfortably manifested. As they are closer to reality based solutions and not faith related prescriptions to cure and overcome complex and twisted mental diseases and other horrifying medical problems facing man.

There are many afflicting problems hurting us, including sadism, and sadistic behaviors, while growing up at no fault of our own and before our 18th birthday, and even at maturity age. Below are to name a few problems facing us that can affect the very core of our being which can victims us for the rest our life, if no professional help could be rendered. With a brief look at history one can realize "superstitious and tyranny" have been two imposing force which have caused frozen minds and backwardness, whenever senseless believes have prevailed. I wonder what would be the role of "sin" in such criteria's as stated below.

Let's first define maturity, and what it should stand for. Maturity is reached when there is a tuneful relationship between a person's body, mind, emotions and spiritual soul under the supervision of their reason and will. And with having access to full mindedness and control of how to make good sense of things. The questions are: Before your 18th birthday, did a parent or other adult in the household occasionally or frequently swear at you're, insulted you, put you down, or humiliate you? OR act in a way that made you frightened that you might be physically hurt, maim, or even killed? Before your 18th birthday, did a parent or other adult in the household occasionally or frequently push, grab, slap, kick, punch, or throw something at you? OR ever hit you so hard that you had marks all over you or were badly injured?

Before your 18th birthday, did an adult or person at least five year older than you ever touch, or fondle you or have you touch their body in a sexual way? OR attempt or actually have oral, anal, or vaginal intercourse with you? Before your 18th birthday, did you occasionally or frequently feel that no one in your family loved you, belittled you or thought you were important or special? OR your family didn't look out for each other, feel close to each other, were acting cold to each other, or support each other?

Before your 18th birthday, did you often or frequently feel that you didn't have enough to eat, had to wear dirty clothes, and had no one to protect you? OR your parents were too drunk or high to take care of you or take you to the doctor if you needed it? Before your 18th birthday, was a biological parent ever lost to you through divorce, abandonment, or other reason, or an orphan, or raised in a single family household.

Before your 18th birthday, was your mother or stepmother often or very often pushed, grabbed, slapped or had something thrown at her? OR sometimes, often, or very often kicked, bitten, hit with a fist, or hit with something hard? OR ever repeatedly hit over at least a few minutes or threatened with a gun or knife? Before your 18th birthday, did you live with anyone who was a problem drinker or alcoholic, a heavy smoker, or who used street drugs? Before your 18th birthday, was a household member depressed or mentally ill, or did a household member attempt suicide, a victim of homicide, or committed homicide? Before your 18th birthday, did a household member go to prison, a felon, under probation, involved in illegal activities?

Before your 18th birthday were you a victim of incest. Before or after your 18th birthday have you ever lived in any sexual prejudice, race, gender prejudice, or xenophobic prejudice, or any other prejudice oriented atmosphere or neighborhood? Before your 18th birthday were you a product of ghetto like environment, and with no education, depleted of having a competent role model in your life and influenced by bad peers flocking together doing bad deeds just to survive or for fun.

Where your prefrontal cortex had to be constructively progressed while growing up reaching maturity and adulthood in a positive and promising atmosphere where good teaching, and professional training would be available, and was not. Before your 18th birthday were you sent to jail, and was introduced to incarceration and ugly punishment, or police brutality, or had a horrifying experience with an inmate or inmates, with not having access to expert therapeutic help, or any other professional counseling's. Before your 18th birthday, or above the age of maturity were you ever a victims of human trafficking, a sex slave treated as a lucrative commodity by notorious organized crime and traffickers, or was sold for monetary gain?

Before your 18th birthday or anytime in your live were you ever so impoverished where you had no choice but to become a victim of prostitution and drug related environment? Before your 18th birthday or any time in your life have you ever been a victim of a gang rape? It does not stop there, abandonment, lack of love and caring, and no compassion, not having proper education, no adequate training, acting on impulse and being instinctual with not having knowledge and acquired wisdom.

Then, we will be prone to decent to irrational behavior which have shown to significantly increase the risk of alcoholism, chronic obstructive pulmonary disease (COPD), depression, fetal death, illicit drug use, ischemic heart disease (IHD), liver disease, risk for intimate partner violence, multiple sexual partners, sexually transmitted diseases, smoking, suicide attempts, unintended pregnancies, early initiation of smoking, early initiation of sexual activity, and adolescent pregnancy, according to the Centers for Disease Control and Prevention (CDC). In Freud's Psychosexual Stages of Development, Freud advanced a theory of personality development that centered on the effects of the sexual pleasure drive on the individual psyche. At particular points in the developmental process, Freud claimed, a single body part is particularly sensitive to sexual, erotic stimulation.

These erogenous zones are the mouth, the anus, and the genital region. The child's libido centers on behavior affecting the primary erogenous zone of his age; he cannot focus on the primary erogenous zone of the next stage without resolving the developmental conflict of the immediate one. When our sexual urges are repressed, it can put us in a difficult position facing dilemmas later on in life. Which obviously no pleading to religious or divine rules can constructively help a sick person no matter how advanced in its hocus-pocus of divine offering for a viable cure or to alleviate pain. And only a sick society is to mass produce perverts, human and sex trafficking, where sex predators are prevalent lurking and inconspicuously awaiting to target vulnerable preys forcing them into prostitution and sex parlors.

There is no needs of such abhorrent behaviors, if the cause and effect to these crucial matters are intelligently, insightfully, scientifically and medically reckoned, deflecting superstitions and shame, and in trying hard to respond to them meaningfully and rationally. Any decent statistics can make it clear that when luck runs out on some people, then they become the victims of a Russian roulette monetary system that can sink them to the very bottom of the barrel with no glimmer of hope. Where doing odd things including selling their bodies is not far-fetched, and sometimes the only option left for their survival. Where the only hope left is for the victims to be made aware of the real culprits to their seemingly hopeless situation, and informed of the potential hazards in taking risk for selling their body either by choice or otherwise.

It is undeniably regretful when sex is literally looked at and taken as a lubricant commodity making billions for notorious organized oriented crimes and their instigators at the cost of so much ignorant and lack of constructive understanding and wellness in the nature of the sexual and economical problem and corruption. It is important to realize a sexual renaissance is of value when accompanied with many awareness and educational places, and thousands of centers for disease control with viable positive planning. Where the basic economic needs of people are met, since so many short lived and temporary sexual interactions and activities are done in exchange of some sort of gift and favor, making such endeared natural feeling to become a monetary game.

We need a modified culture of accepting sexual revolution where people are not to sell themselves as commodities, but truly seeing it as a gift from divine to be enjoyed, and to opt themselves out from taking it with a guilty conscious, or a sin and amoral. we need to stop malicious persecution of those people left with no choice either financially or emotionally since they are wickedly punished if caught in the act of sex so to speak illegally making sex retribution a social norm which also gives birth to honor killing and other insidious crimes done against the victims.

The punishment must be directed towards those who design criteria's of exploiting desperate human being for money, and not the actual victims in search of a way out of their miserable and very difficult condition that are either emotionally in love, or financially desperate. It is unfortunately the poor that are worse off the most, when caught in the web of such proactive feelings, and back warded cultural thinking, with financial shortcomings which sometimes leads to inferiority complex, and mental problems and incompetence's. Since many are devoid of education, wealth, and a luxury living flared- up with financial faculty, power, influence or fame, and are considered not worth knowing by today's standard. And since these prominent attributes are exclusive, and not inclusive, and the building blocks of a monetary system, where wealth, power and influence dictate.

Bear in mind that these status quo of unfortunate and seemingly irresolvable situations look ominous, but they are opportunities in disguise that should be cultivated and capitalized on. People of misfortune can create miracle if only leveraged to awaken the elephant within and with little encouragement from able bodies and role models with little support from a caring system or government, where they are not deserted and left desolate like remote islands, if so, every one of us can reach stars. I believe: "the tighter the spring the higher the jump." No matter what are the deficiencies in our life a spur to awakening, with some therapeutic help and encouragement, and constructive guidance can propel so far in dynamically changing one's life for the better, beyond belief? Be it sex related depravity and challenges, psychosexual difficulties, financial problems, mental and spiritual anxieties, physical shortcomings, or any other problem.

We ought to know we all are carrying a tender box called brain, which needs to be lid, and if truly awakened and enlightened, one can conquer the world and beyond, since plenty of icons already have challenged the physical and the mental and financial barriers, and have overcome capricious and seemingly difficult position and have reached their mountain top despite seemingly insurmountable obstacles.

Any decent statistics can make it clear that when luck runs out on some people, then they become the victims of a Russian roulette monetary system that can sink them to the very bottom of the barrel with no glimmer of hope. Where doing odd things including selling their bodies is not far-fetched, and sometimes the only option left for their survival. What I am saying is sexual needs are potently interlaced in our biology which are undeniable fact of our desires and psyche. And when financial depravities are weaved in with illiteracy and lack of professional training. Then, there are times when these can make one vulnerable to so called prostitution, such an ugly term for some left with no choice. Which can make victims to carry guilty conscious and are finger pointed as being sinful.

Since there are no open-mindedness and awareness to the root causes of the actual trouble being manifested, where sometimes people are horrifyingly prosecuted by the very same system incompetent of providing employment and also education where these normal urges would not be seen as dilemmas but accepted as undeniable fact of our life. Instead of labeling these natural feelings and urges for abnormal behaviors which certainly are the byproduct of ruse and wrong tradition, and also the system's shortcoming in economic management and programming.

With no leniency of being assisted with decisive therapeutic and appropriate financial social remedies, and proper employment. Why not develop thousands of meaningful developing and educational centers. Creating millions of good paying jobs for hired professional in related field to save souls not to be wasted. Where there are positive and potential human resources in households with illiteracies, stricken with poverty, anxiety, hence discouraged and dismayed. Which they could have a way out of their miserable life, and could be given a chance to stop the bucket of poverty and its cynicism where it must.

In advanced societies this issue is mitigated to a point where they realize there are bad consequences to not having an efficient economy or not able to manage the forces of the market, and with no adequate and systematic way of dealing with sexual culture and interactions in their societies. Which any expert in dealing with human emotion and sex can attest to it as being wrong, and in need of a constructive revolution of thought and behavior. Since sex should be educatory redefined, understood, and prevalent to new norms.

In conclusion many of social ill and hurdles facing people can be mitigated especially in developing countries, if progressive and liberated culture of thinking could take place. Where dark ages of responding with cruelty to vital human feeling and relationships could become relaxed and not so stiffened. Since there is still a wide gap and huge discrepancies between traditionally cultured social norms and the liberty in expressing true sexual feeling and coming out of closet. Where many approach to love and sex is bombarded with wrong propaganda which certainly tempts, and negatively affect masses of people with sex and porn addiction, and other inappropriate sexual issues. Because it is seen as a lucrative commodity, therefore enticing many impoverished people to engage in sexual undertakings for money. With sometimes having no choice, since they are also tricked into deceitful promises and then taken advantage of by rogue and notorious crime organizations, and drug pushers. These sexual predators are the real menace to society where they prey on helpless and naïve souls for monetary transaction and exchange where there is no limit to their atrocities and charlatanism.

I believe congressional and international body should assemble to discuss and to establish new charters on human rights targeting many governments to avoid despotic behaviors against their own citizens and put the blame where it needs to be. And since noble and scholarly authorities must question cultural backwardness of stoning people, and forced marriages for the sake of financial gain, forced child spousal and abuse. And not to tolerate prejudices, and to avoid finger pointing and labeling people with sin.

Those responsible for such atrocity of conduct should be held accountable where they must stop ruthlessly prosecuting individuals that are in the bottom of the barrel; with no hope left but to risk their lives selling their bodies to make the bare minimum of living, and are emotionally entangled in a web of uncertainties without any guidance available to them leading them to sex and so called prostitution. And perhaps are obsessed with feeling and in love, which in many cases their rendezvous can turn into disaster if caught, where these punishing rules from dark ages are legally implemented by law.

DHAMMAPADA believed quote: "Whomever harms the harmless and offends the inoffensive, he will come to one of these misfortunes: he will have suffering, great loss, injury, sever illness, madness or trouble with authorities."

Should Animals be punished?

I sometimes wonder, what is it that makes us certain and so sure to decide what is wrong and what is right? And if our unanimous consent and agreements should sometimes be morally challenged, if they are not righteously justified. But sometimes issues become intricately difficult, in which they reach a realm beyond our cognitive ability and true understanding, and since making us incompetent to deliver them wisely and correctly. I try to make it as less controversial as possible, since It occurred to me when animals do wrong and cause some sorts of injury to humans, or cause other kinds of mishaps. We are to put them to sleep, and get rid of them.

We do not consider other clinical or therapeutically options for animals, because we believe that animals do not have the potential to see the difference and are not able to substantiate good behavior or to improve noticeably. So that we would not be in harm's way and to avoid becoming the victim of their future harm. Furthermore, they do not have the brains for it and they act instinctively by nature. I am also marveled, and wonder how God would punish animals if and when they do wrong and cause harm after they die. Or should he really punish them? After all he is a just, and all powerful, omnipotent, omnipresent, and a lovable god.

Why should he punish these creatures if they do not know any better? As they do not possesses the wit to distinguish between what is wrong and what is right. And why some humans should be punished if they do not know any better either. Especially when there are available options with alternatives that make it possible for them to be trained, and seek professional help that certainly would be effective; in making wrong doers better persons, since it would improve the quality of their character and behaviors, but we do not, and if we do, it is certainly done haphazardly, and sure not decisive and good enough.

It is a choice that is not available to animals, and I like to know if it is fair for our almighty God to punish human wrong doers after they die, as they did not know any better. That could have occurred because of no knowledge, and lack of education opportunities which should have been available to them to improve themselves in becoming much better characters and good human beings, but they had not and since were deprived of a meaningful life.

Do you not think those who are in charge of our natural resources, and our economy, those who govern, and do have access to power, and can hugely influence anything and most everything in our life? Should care and furnish more training, expertise, and positive life changing and professional help for indigents and the helpless. Since there is a tight correlation between poverty, lack of education and crime, in which if they could be assisted with glimpse of hope and learning, it could turn them into a better citizens so that perhaps less people would end up imprison, and sent to electric chairs? Abigail Adams says quote: "Learning is not attained by chance, it must be sought for with ardor, and attended with diligent." Could you tell me who is really at fault, and whom should God really punish after they die, those with overwhelming ability, money, power and influence? As they can change people's life for the better with a stroke of a pen, but they choose not, or those whom sleep dinner less every night, and cannot discern right from wrong, having a nomadic education, or none at all, compounded with the pain of seeing their loved ones hungry, and with no shelter or medicine available to them.

Tell me if the most primitive societies, and the most advanced should react the same in punishing the propagators of the same crimes and for them to receive similar capital punishments. Then what is really the difference, when we call other less developed nations barbaric, and saying it proudly and with pride. Wouldn't that be just bragging and acting pompous, and irresponsible? Should we not think, this is hypocrisy in deed, and only true in empty rhetoric?

Since poverty also has a lot to do with many violators breaking the law, and act criminal? Relieve people's financial pain, and let the good grow? Let the Godly and divine parts of human beings to flourish, show them there is light at the end of the tunnel, and mean it, because they are so marginalized and inhumanly treated, with no food as many die a quiet death, like they never existed.

Life is meant to be good, but it sure requires balance, no one would be better off, and every one eventually becomes worse off when collective goodness is ignored. And I am sure anyone with a little compassion would say, no the animals should not be punished since they do not know any better, we should seek some humane solution to this literal and gigantic problem. This elephant of poverty and no education in the room cannot be ignored, it is the root cause of all evils.

why should those people who were never given a chance to learn, and in most cases were the victims of horrifying crimes themselves, and since, they became forlorn (miserable), should be penalized with capital punishment when they do wrong. Because if we appropriately deal with human nature and nurture, and in taking preventive measures in them doing wrong by educating, and to spur people to the right direction, it sure can make a huge positive difference in their life, since the right training is a science that must be taken serious, and should not be foregone through negligent and default. Chinese Proverb says quote: "Tell me and I'll forget; show me and I may remember; involve me and I'll understand." And I like to add human being curiosity should preemptively be stirred to the right direction, especially when still immature and in its infancy.

The Vital Role of Bodily Hormones and Endocrine Glands

Can hormones make you healthy and happy? Yes, but then if one is not eating wholesome food, not having enough and good rest, and if mentally exhausted since one has to deal with family and work oriented problems, and so on. Then these natural and beneficial hormones not only would not help, they will have adverse effect where one can be at great risk. Emerging field of contemplative psychology, including bio cognitive, and Neuro psychology in concert with cognitive science and medical anthropology, and many other advanced medical entities, believe external and anxiety driven stimuli effect our mental and cerebral ability, which interplays a huge role in impacting our bodily health and our wellbeing's.

Our feelings and our emotions are constantly challenged and influenced by external stimuli, and sometimes not controlled variables. Which in return can exude more of some bodily hormones, or less; which, either way, it can leave a dire effect in our body, since they are not balanced. Chemical reactions spur us to behave in different ways, feeling good, bad, excited, feeling hungry, angry, to feel resentful, feel in love, feeling friendly, feel optimistic and hopeful, or pessimistic, feeling sad and melancholy, stressed, fearful, feeling anxiety and distressed, cornered and lonely, feeling vengeful, even effecting our physical stature of tall and how short one is, and so on. They can cause a host of deadly diseases, like auto immune disease, cancer, strokes and heart attacks, sexual impotencies, and so on, which directly correlated with one feeling bad, and sometimes being finger pointed because of cultural taboos, and stricken with shame of not belonging, diving good souls with depression and sometimes to the verge of committing suicide, which even push some people to commit homicide and to enact killing spree.

If chemical interactions and hormonal mechanism act properly, and maintained with balance, then they can function appropriately, which then, many hormones, and electrical impulses in our body will assist us to tolerate difficult and unexpected situation. These chemical substances in our body are made by endocrine glands which release hormones into our blood, this is why they can affect us in many ways. For example "Serotonin" is called the "happy hormone" which regulates our mood, makes us happy and prevents depression. Serotonin can be released by getting exposed to sunlight, by eating foods rich in carbohydrates and by exercising. "Endorphin': Endorphins can make you feel good, reduce anxiety and our sensitivity to pain, Endorphins are released by exercising. "Dopamine": Dopamine helps you to feel mentally alert. The lack of it might cause lack of attention, lack of concentration and bad moods.

Dopamine can be released by eating foods that are rich in protein. "Phenylethamine": Phenylethamine is the hormone that results in the feelings we get in the early stages of a relationship. Cocoa beans contain Phenylethamine. Eating chocolate might be helpful too. (See why woman love chocolate so much) "Ghrelin": Ghrelin is a hormone that reduces stress and can help you become more relaxed. Ghrelin is released when we become Hungary that's why eating too much is not always a good idea. Just eat according to your body's needs and never fill your stomach completely in order to maintain good Ghrelin levels. "Adrenal hormone."

The human body possess two adrenal glands and one sits on top of each kidney, and each adrenal gland weighs about five grams in adult. These glands secrete several hormone which act as "chemical messenger." Where the hormones travel in our blood stream and act on various body tissues to enable them function correctly.

All adrenocortical hormone are "steroid compounds" derived from cholesterol. Among several hormones that adrenal glands produces, the one that is predominantly "cortisol" deals with stress respond, and also helps to regulate body metabolism. And when one or a beloved is under pressure or perhaps in a fearful and life threatening position of any kind. It is noteworthy to realize that a very strong factor that can make a huge difference in a life and death situation is our adrenal hormone. Which exudes from our adrenal glands since facing such emergency and alarming criterion where secretion automatically takes place enabling one to become keenly alerted and to make "the fight or flight applicable."

This very potent hormone is the strongest force known to man which naturally exudes when one is truly frightened or distressed with facing an emergency status. This miracle like agent will not be a benefactor to culprit and the proponent of the violence since he or she is the one causing such horrifying atmosphere and therefore not the one petrified and or at risk of being the victim of a heinous crime which is about to happen. If this miracle like hormone that is available at any emergency and crucial time realized and consequently leveraged. It will make the victim to fight back defending oneself or loved ones with all of one's might that we perhaps take for granted.

We should take advantage of such natural amenities when in real danger and replace our fear with this potent energy force which most definitely could make a difference in a radical and scary environment and can help to save lives. And if you ever wondered that tasks sometimes beyond believe happen with outstanding courage, and superb human resiliency, be reminded of this wonderful and marvelous hormone. It is good to know the reason to why they are called adrenal gland, because they lie on top of kidneys. A small amount of adrenaline is produced and this helps to maintain normal blood pressure. In situation of stress, however, where the body might be involved in a "fight or flight" a large amount of adrenaline is produce very quickly which dramatically effects the body.

Adrenaline raises blood sugar stimulating the liver to change glycogen into glucose, caused by fatty tissue to release fat into blood. It increases heart rate, increase blood flow to the muscles, reduces blood flow to the skin and intestine, and transfers blood into the limbic system to be more active. It widens bronchioles, and dilates the pupil. All of this means the body is ready for action.

It is of concern when in our stressful life which because of too much stress a large amount of adrenalin also exudes. Which can be harmful since our sedentary life style is also adds to the problem, then, giving more chance to these miracle like hormone to cause harm. Many of life episode can disproportionately affect the release of such hormone, stress caused by family problems, unemployment and having to deal with expenses, and too many bills, exams, even the headaches of traffics jams, and having to deal with too much bureaucracies, and red tapes, and environmental problems. Even name callings, belittling others, and suppressing their hopes and desire, threatening them, discriminating against them, bulling, inhibiting anyone from exploring their talent and their right to express themselves, and stopping people from freedom of assembly, freedom of speech, or denying them freedom of press, and religious, can definitely impact people for worse, psychologically, physically and within killing their spirit, and so to speak driving them up the wall, another world making them insane.

It is very wise to know, and to maintain balance into our life, and seek peace and tranquility of mind and behaviors so that not only we can be more safe and also coexist with others in a humanly way. "The growth hormone": is a complicated process and needs the coordination of several hormones which the main one is the growth hormone. It is produced by pituitary gland and acts on the liver, stimulating it to produce another hormone.

It is the secondary hormone which directly effects the growth of the bone and muscle. Growth hormone also helps to control the body use of protein, carbohydrates, and fat. In babies if growth hormone is not produced enough, this can result in "dwarfism." The treatment for deficiency is to give child growth hormone, which now days is produced by genetic engineering. If too much growth hormones is produced in child then "Gigantism" results, and too much growth hormone in adult results in a disease called "acromegaly" in which there is overgrowth in bones giving the person a change of appearance; this occurs gradually over a long period of time.

Genetic engineering means there is a plentiful supply of growth hormone for everyone that needs it. Growth hormone might also have role in anti-aging treatment. The cow version "Bovine" growth hormone and the pig version "porcine" growth hormone have been used in animals to increase yields of milk and leaner meet. The "pancreas" makes insulin which regulates the level of sugar in the blood. "Thyroids gland" makes "thyroxin, which gives over all control of the rate of chemical processes in our body which is called the metabolic rate. The "ovaries" produce female sex hormones including "progesterone, and estrogen" which control body changes at puberty and during menstrual cycle.

When the ovaries start to produce egg menstruation starts. Sex hormones are responsible for dramatic changes that happens in the body. They control puberty egg and sperm production, birth, and lactation (breast feeding), also responsible for pregnancy. If a fertilized egg starts to grow in the uterus, then, the woman is pregnant, and her periods stops.

This occurs since during pregnancy "progesterone" continue to be produced which maintains the thicker lining of the uterus and stops the development of any more egg in the ovaries. At birth and breast feeding hormones are once again activated in the birth process. When the baby has been growing for about nine month, the pituitary gland produces a hormone called "oxytocin" which starts contraction of uterus. At birth the level of progesterone falls and the pituitary produces another hormone which causes the production of milk. "Oxytocin and prolactin" are involved in ejection of milk from the breast and continue production of milk throughout pregnancy "The testes" produces male sex hormones including "testosterone" which control body changes at puberty and also sperm production. ADH (anti-diuretic- hormone).

The amount of water in the blood must be kept more or less the same all the same at a normal level at all the time. So there has to be a balance between the amount of water taken in the diet and the amount of lost by the body in sweeting, evaporating, faces, and urine. This is achieved by action of the (ADH) hormone. For example you have not drunk for a while or you have been sweeting a lot. Part of the brain the "hypothalamus" detects that there is not enough water in the blood. The hypothalamus sends a message to the pituitary, which releases ADH. Then travels in the blood to the kidneys which saves water, so that the urine become less in the volume, and more concentrated.

The level of water in the blood can then begin to rise and the water is ingested and produced by the process of respiration. If there is too high level of water in the blood because for example it is too cold and you have not been losing any water through sweeting, the hypothalamus sends a message to the pituitary gland and production of (ADH) will stop. The kidney will not save as much water and the urine becomes diluted and of great volume.

The level of water in the blood then begins to fall towards the ideal level. This is an example of negative feedback. As the level of the water in the blood falls, feedback ensures that the amount of (ADH) rises. As the level of water in the blood rises feedback ensures that the amount of (ADH) falls. Alcohol can decrease the amount of (ADH) being produced resulting in a greater volume of more dilute urine being produced. This can lead to dehydration. Ecstasy has the opposite effect, that is, ecstasy increases the amount (ADH) which reduces the amount of urine produced. Both alcohol and ecstasy interfere with the normal regulation of water in the body and may be harmful long term effecting body.

At the end one should ask: if our mind influences our health and wellbeing's—but then, what's influencing our mind? And I tell you a host of external stimuli, the impact of either a stressful life or a good live, which each in turn can most definitely leave its foot print on our body, our mind and soul, which is either for better or for worse.

We ought to know the food we eat, needs to be wholesome, and not junk food, and having restful nights should be taken seriously; type of work we do will affect us, peer pressure, and the people we associate with, family and friend which we deal with, our environment and the type of upbringing we are involved in, and certainly the financial life style we are entangled with, and most of all, how positive and hopeful we are in our life. Can sure make a huge impact in all of which we undertake and a very decisive role in our future. Optimally one should try not to feel pessimistic and gloomy, and should be patient and proactive in the midst of turmoil and mishaps facing them, should be passionate about living a good live. And if one is reluctant to change one's life for better, one should at least not put off, and or procrastinate to make a habit of reading, and to think positive, do not let despair overcome you, it will be the end of you. One should exercise, and be active in all of which one loves to do, try to diversify and be creative, stay away from having too much monotonous activities, it will depress you, and stay far away from being sedentary and keep moving. Since all of the above can proportionately influence trillions of living cell, with having mind of their own, which are very alert to our pleasant circumstances, or ill situations. Because they immediately respond to our mental and physical boom or gloom, to either release constructive happy and healthy hormone into our blood stream which directly affects us, or relinquishing otherwise, toxic hormone making our life miserable, and perhaps destructive.

And again I stress, you are what you eat, you are what you think, you are what you believe, you are what you do and how you behave, you are what you say, and you are a huge leap into what God made possible. And preeminently, you cannot reach God and humanity by your thoughts alone, since monkey business is sometimes associated with mind; it can only take you so far, you must connect to God and others through the purity of your heart, it is just a different world with an unequal realm of existence.

We ought to remember that: every harsh and hateful saying, will be recorded by your subconscious mind and to whom you addressed it to, like a memory archive on computer where files are preserved. Because human beings are all about emotion, bitter words can pierce through our soul with no hesitancy, where toxic hormone become released, referencing our anger and rage, and the more we repeat them nasty and threatening words intestinally or not, and the more they register, which gradually hypnotize us to believe, and deliver and to act upon what we rightfully or not uttered repeatedly, which can eventually haunt us, and sometimes for the worse.

About the Author

Dr. Feridoun Shawn Shahmoradian earned a bachelor's degree in electronic engineering technology from Texas Southern University, a master's degree in economics from Texas A&M University, and a master's in public administration from University of Texas at Dallas. He teaches martial arts and lives with his wife in Houston, Texas.

Printed in the United States
By Bookmasters